God's Promises®
for Your Every Need
Catholic Edition

God's Promises®
for Your Every Need
Catholic Edition

Edited by

Sr. Mary Ann Strain, C.P.
Rev. Victor Hoagland, C.P..

Regina Press
New York

Nihil Obstat: Reverend Charles Caccavale, S.T.D.
                   Censor librorum
                   February 24, 2004

Imprimatur: Most Reverend William Murphy
                   Bishop of Rockville Centre
                   March 1, 2004

Cover design by Uttley/DouPonce DesignWorks, Sisters, Oregon.

Compiled by Dr. A. L. Gill.

ISBN# 0-88271-072-9

Printed in the United States of America.

THE REGINA PRESS
10 Hub Drive
Melville, New York 11747

∞ Contents ∞

Jesus Is Your . . .

The Bible is Your . . .

What to Do When You Feel . . .

What to Do When You Are . . .

What to Do When . . .

What the Bible Has to Say About . . .

Truth from the Bible About . . .

What You Can Do to . . .

Jesus Is Your . . .
Savior ✍

Not because of any righteous deeds
    we had done
but because of his mercy,
he saved us through the bath of rebirth
and renewal by the holy Spirit,
whom he richly poured out on us
through Jesus Christ our savior.

Titus 3:5-6

Moreover, we have seen and testify that the Father sent his Son as savior of the world.

1 John 4:14

My spirit rejoices in God my savior.

Luke 1:47

We have heard for ourselves, and we know that this is truly the savior of the world.

John 4:42b

For the Son of Man has come to seek and to save what was lost.

Luke 19:10

For God so loved the world that he gave his only Son, so that everyone who believes in him might not perish but might have eternal life.

John 3:16

But God, who is rich in mercy, because of the great love he had for us, even when we were dead in our transgressions, brought us to life with Christ (by grace you have been saved).

Ephesians 2:4-5

For by grace you have been saved through faith, and this is not from you; it is the gift of God; it is not from works, so no one may boast.

Ephesians 2:8-9

For, if you confess with your mouth that Jesus is Lord and believe in your heart that God raised him from the dead, you will be saved.

Romans 10:9

Jesus Is Your . . .
Lord ✑

For, if you confess with your mouth that Jesus is Lord and believe in your heart that God raised him from the dead, you will be saved. For one believes with the heart and so is justified, and one confesses with the mouth and so is saved.

Romans 10:9-10

For sin is not to have any power over you, since you are not under the law but under grace.

What then? Shall we sin because we are not under the law but under grace? Of course not! Do you not know that if you present yourselves to someone as obedient slaves, you are slaves of the one you obey, either of sin, which leads to death, or of obedience, which leads to righteousness?

Romans 6:14-16

Do you not know that your body is a temple of the holy Spirit within you, whom you have from God, and that you are not your own? For you have been purchased at a price. Therefore glorify God in your body.

1 Corinthians 6:19-20

Therefore let the whole house of Israel know for certain that God has made him both Lord and Messiah, this Jesus whom you crucified.

Acts 2:36

For if we live, we live for the Lord, and if we die, we die for the Lord; so then, whether we live or die, we are the Lord's.

Romans 14:8

Blessed be the Lord day by day,
　God, our salvation, who carries us.

Psalm 68:20

You shall love the Lord your God with all your heart, with all your soul, with all your mind, and with all your strength.

Mark 12:30

Jesus Is Your . . .
Love ✍

But God proves his love for us in that while we were still sinners Christ died for us.

Romans 5:8

For God so loved the world that he gave his only Son, so that everyone who believes in him might not perish but might have eternal life.

John 3:16

Beloved let us love one another, because love is of God; everyone who loves is begotten by God and knows God. Whoever is without love does not know God, for God is love. In this way the love of God was revealed to us: God sent his only Son into the world so that we might have life through him. In this is love: not that we have loved God, but that he loved us and sent his Son as expiation for our sins. Beloved, if God so loved us, we also must love one another. No one has ever seen God. Yet, if we love one another, God remains in us, and his love is brought to perfection in us.

1 John 4:7-12

We have come to know and to believe in the

love God has for us.

God is love, and whoever remains in love remains in God and God in him. We love because he first loved us.

1 John 4:16, 19

As the Father loves me, so I also love you. Remain in my love. If you keep my commandments, you will remain in my love, just as I have kept my Father's commandments and remain in his love.

I have told you this so that my joy might be in you and your joy might be complete. This is my commandment: love one another as I love you. No one has greater love than this, to lay down one's life for one's friends. This I command you: love one another.

John 15:9-13, 17

Whoever has my commandments and observes them is the one who loves me. And whoever loves me will be loved by my Father, and I will love him and reveal myself to him.

John 14:21

So faith, hope, love remain, these three; but the greatest of these is love.

1 Corinthians 13:13

For I am convinced that neither death, nor life, nor angels, nor principalities, nor present things, nor future things, nor powers, nor height, nor depth, nor any other creature will be able to separate us from the love of God in Christ Jesus our Lord.

Romans 8:38-39

Jesus Is Your . . .
Peace ❧

But now in Christ Jesus you who once were far off have become near by the blood of Christ.

For he is our peace, he who made both one and broke down the dividing wall of enmity, through his flesh.

Ephesians 2:13-14

Keep on doing what you have learned and received and heard and seen in me. Then the God of peace will be with you.

Philippians 4:9

Therefore, since we have been justified by faith, we have peace with God through our Lord Jesus Christ.

Romans 5:1

And let the peace of Christ control your hearts, the peace into which you were also called in one body. And be thankful.

Colossians 3:15

May the LORD give might to his people;
    may the LORD bless his people with peace!

Psalm 29:11

Peace I leave with you; my peace I give to you. Not as the world gives do I give it to you. Do not let your hearts be troubled or afraid.

John 14:27

Have no anxiety at all, but in everything, by prayer and petition, with thanksgiving, make your requests known to God. Then the peace of God that surpasses all understanding will guard your hearts and minds in Christ Jesus.

Philippians 4:6-7

Jesus Is Your . . .
Forgiveness ✍

In love he destined us for adoption to himself through Jesus Christ, in accordance with the favor of his will, for the praise of the glory of his grace that he granted us in the beloved.

In him we have redemption by his blood, the forgiveness of transgressions, in accord with the riches of his grace. that he lavished upon us.

Ephesians 1:4-8

So whoever is in Christ is a new creation: the old things have passed away; behold, new things have come.

2 Corinthians 5:17

My children, I am writing this to you so that you may not commit sin. But if anyone does sin, we have an Advocate with the Father, Jesus Christ the righteous one.

1 John 2:1

If we acknowledge our sins, he is faithful and just and will forgive our sins and cleanse us from every wrongdoing.

1 John 1:9

For I will forgive their evildoing
and remember their sins no more.

Hebrews 8:12

Put on then, as God's chesen ones, holy and beloved, heartfelt compassion, kindness, humility, gentleness, and patience, bearing with one another and forgiving one another, if one has a grievance against another; as the Lord has forgiven you, so must you also do.

Colossians 3:12-13

When you stand to pray, forgive anyone against whom you have a grievance, so that your heavenly Father may in turn forgive you your transgressions.

Mark 11:25

It is I, I, who wipe out,
    for my own sake, your offenses;
    your sins I remember no more.

Isaiah 43:25

Happy the sinner whose fault is removed,
    whose sin is forgiven.
Happy those to whom the LORD imputes
        no guilt,
    in whose spirit is no deceit.

Psalm 32:1-2

Jesus Is Your . . .
Holiness ✍

For our sake he made him to be sin who did not
know sin, so that we might become the
righteousness of God in him.

2 Corinthians 5:21

It is due to him that you are in Christ Jesus, who
became for us wisdom from God, as well as
righteousness, sanctification, and redemption.

1 Corinthians 1:30

Thus Abraham "believed God, and it was
credited to him as righteousness."

Realize then that it is those who have faith who
are children of Abraham.

Galatians 3:6-7

But now the righteousness of God has been
manifested apart from the law, though testified to
by the law and the prophets, the righteousness of
God through faith in Jesus Christ for all who
believe.

Romans 3:21-22

They are justified freely by his grace through
the redemption in Christ Jesus, whom God set forth

as an expiation, through faith, by his blood, to prove his righteousness because of the forgiveness of sins previously committed, through the forbearance of God--to prove his righteousness in the present time, that he might be righteous and justify the one who has faith in Jesus.

Romans 3:24-26

Not because of any righteous deeds we had
> done
but because of his mercy,
he saved us through the bath of rebirth
and renewal by the holy Spirit,

Titus 3:5

For what the law, weakened by the flesh, was powerless to do, this God has done: by sending his own Son in the likeness of sinful flesh and for the sake of sin, he condemned sin in the flesh, so that the righteous decree of the law might be fulfilled in us, who live not according to the flesh but according to the spirit.

Romans 8:3-4

What then shall we say? That Gentiles, who did not pursue righteousness, have achieved it, that is, righteousness that comes from faith.

Romans 9:30

But if Christ is in you, although the body is dead because of sin, the spirit is alive because of righteousness.

Romans 8:10

Justice will bring about peace;
    right will produce calm and security.

Isaiah 32:17

In justice shall you be established,
  far from the fear of oppression,
  where destruction cannot come near you.
Should there be any attack, it shall
      not be of my making;
  whoever attacks you shall fall before you.
Lo, I have created the craftsman
  who blows on the burning coals
  and forges weapons as his work;
It is I also who have created
  the destroyer to work havoc.
No weapon fashioned against you
      shall prevail;
  every tongue you shall prove false
  that launches an accusation against you.
This is the lot of the servants of the LORD,
  their vindication from me, says the LORD.

Isaiah 54:14-17

Jesus Is Your . . .
Deliverer ᔓ

And you will know the truth, and the truth will set you free. So if a son frees you, then you will truly be free.

John 8:32, 36

For the law of the spirit of life in Christ Jesus has freed you from the law of sin and death.

Romans 8:2

Now the Lord is the Spirit, and where the Spirit of the Lord is, there is freedom.

2 Corinthians 3:17

But now that you have been freed from sin and have become slaves of God, the benefit that you have leads to sanctification, and its end is eternal life.

Romans 6:22

For every boot that tramped in battle,
    every cloak rolled in blood,
    will be burned as fuel for flames.

Isaiah 9:4

The Spirit of the Lord is upon me,
  because he has anointed me
    to bring glad tidings to the poor.
He has sent me to proclaim liberty
    to captives
  and recovery of sight to the blind,
    to let the oppressed go free.

Luke 4:18

Behold, I have given you the power 'to tread upon serpents' and scorpions and upon the full force of the enemy and nothing will harm you.

Luke 10:19

Beloved, do not trust every spirit but test the spirits to see whether they belong to God, because many false prophets have gone out into the world. This is how you can know the Spirit of God: every spirit that acknowledges Jesus Christ come in the flesh belongs to God, and every spirit that does not acknowledge Jesus does not belong to God. This is the spirit of the antichrist that, as you heard, is to come, but in fact is already in the world. You belong to God, children, and you have conquered them, for the one who is in you is greater than the one who is in the world.

1 John 4:1-4

Jesus Is Your . . .
Friend ✍

God is faithful, and by him you were called to fellowship with his Son, Jesus Christ our Lord.

1 Corinthians 1:9

Behold, I stand at the door and knock. If anyone hears my voice and opens the door, [then] I will enter his house and dine with him, and he with me.

Revelation 3:20

Jesus answered and said to him, "Whoever loves me will keep my word, and my Father will love him, and we will come to him and make our dwelling with him."

John 14:23

Sing and rejoice, O daughter Zion! See, I am coming to dwell among you, says the LORD.

Zechariah 2:14

For where two or three are gathered together in my name, there am I in the midst of them.

Matthew 18:20

Whoever has my commandments and observes them is the one who loves me. And whoever loves me will be loved by my Father, and I will love him and reveal myself to him.

John 14:21

I am the friend of all who fear you,
of all who keep your precepts.

Psalm 119:63

And live in love, as Christ loved us and handed himself over for us as a sacrificial offering to God for a fragrant aroma...addressing one another [in] psalms and hymns and spiritual songs, singing and playing to the Lord in your hearts...because we are members of his body.

Ephesians 5:2, 19, 30

Now this is the message that we have heard from him and proclaim to you: God is light, and in him there is no darkness at all. If we say, "We have fellowship with him," while we continue to walk in darkness, we lie and do not act in truth. But if we walk in the light as he is in the light, then we have fellowship with one another, and the blood of his Son Jesus cleanses us from all sin.

1 John 1:5-7

Jesus Is Your . . .
Example ❧

For to this you have been called, because Christ also suffered for you, leaving you an example that you should follow in his footsteps.

1 Peter 2:21

Whoever claims to abide in him ought to live [just] as he lived.

1 John 2:6

So be imitators of God, as beloved children, and live in love, as Christ loved us and handed himself over for us as a sacrificial offering to God for a fragrant aroma.

Ephesians 5:1-2

But it shall not be so among you. Rather, whoever wishes to be great among you will be your servant; whoever wishes to be first among you will be the slave of all. For the Son of Man did not come to be served but to serve and to give his life as a ransom for many.

Mark 10:43-45

If I, therefore, the master and teacher, have

washed your feet, you ought to wash one another's feet. I have given you a model to follow, so that as I have done for you, you should also do.

John 13:14-15

I give you a new commandment: love one another. As I have loved you, so you also should love one another.

John 13:34

The way we came to know love was that he laid down his life for us; so we ought to lay down our lives for our brothers.

1 John 3:16

Put on then, as God's chosen ones, holy and beloved, heartfelt compassion, kindness, humility, gentleness, and patience, bearing with one another and forgiving one another, if one has a grievance against another; as the Lord has forgiven you, so must you also do.

Colossians 3:12-13

Jesus Is Your . . .
Companion ✍

I am the friend of all who fear you,
of all who keep your precepts.

Psalm 119:63

Some friends bring ruin on us,
but a true friend is more loyal than a brother.

Proverbs 18:24

I no longer call you slaves, because a slave does not know what his master is doing. I have called you friends, because I have told you everything I have heard from my Father. It was not you who chose me, but I who chose you and appointed you to go and bear fruit that will remain, so that whatever you ask the Father in my name he may give you.

John 15:15-16

But if we walk in the light as he is in the light, then we have fellowship with one another, and the blood of his Son Jesus cleanses us from all sin.

1 John 1:7

Draw near to God, and he will draw near to

you. Cleanse your hands, you sinners, and purify your hearts, you of two minds.

James 4:8

Even if my father and mother forsake me,
    the LORD will take me in.

Psalm 27:10

You are my friends if you do what I command you.

John 15:14

God is faithful, and by him you were called to fellowship with his Son, Jesus Christ our Lord.

1 Corinthians 1:9

I will not leave you orphans; I will come to you.

John 14:18

Jesus Is Your . . .
Brother ✍

For whoever does the will of my heavenly Father is my brother, and sister, and mother.

Matthew 12:50

He who consecrates and those who are being consecrated all have one origin. Therefore, he is not ashamed to call them "brothers."

Hebrews 2:11

For those he foreknew he also predestined to be conformed to the image of his Son, so that he might be the firstborn among many brothers.

Romans 8:29

So then you are no longer strangers and sojourners, but you are fellow citizens with the holy ones and members of the household of God.

Ephesians 2:19

See what love the Father has bestowed on us that we may be called the children of God. Yet so we are. The reason the world does not know us is that it did not know him.

1 John 3:1

As proof that you are children, God sent the spirit of his Son into our hearts, crying out, "Abba, Father!" So you are no longer a slave but a child, and if a child then also an heir, through God.

Galatians 4:6-7

Beloved, we are God's children now; what we shall be has not yet been revealed. We do know that when it is revealed we shall be like him, for we shall see him as he is.

1 John 3:2

Jesus Is Your . . .
Guardian ✍

But you, LORD, are a shield around me;
    my glory, you keep my head high.

Psalm 3:4

But the Lord is faithful; he will strengthen you
and guard you from the evil one.

2 Thessalonians 3:3

He will guard the footsteps of his faithful ones,
    but the wicked shall perish in the darkness.
For not by strength does man prevail.

1 Samuel 2:9

For you are my refuge,
    a tower of strength against the foe.

Psalm 61:4

For the eyes of the Lord are on the righteous
    and his ears turned to their prayer,
but the face of the Lord is against evildoers.
    Now who is going to harm you if you are
enthusiastic for what is good?

1 Peter 3:12-13

Jesus Is Your . . .
Security ✍

My sheep hear my voice; I know them, and they follow me. I give them eternal life, and they shall never perish. No one can take them out of my hand. My Father, who has given them to me, is greater than all, and no one can take them out of the Father's hand.

John 10:27-29

For I am convinced that neither death, nor life, nor angels, nor principalities, nor present things, nor future things, nor powers, nor height, nor depth, nor any other creature will be able to separate us from the love of God in Christ Jesus our Lord.

Romans 8:38-39

But the Lord is faithful; he will strengthen you and guard you from the evil one.

2 Thessalonians 3:3

Everything that the Father gives me will come to me, and I will not reject anyone who comes to me.

John 6:37

Do not work for food that perishes but for the food that endures for eternal life, which the Son of Man will give you. For on him the Father, God, has set his seal.

John 6:27

In him you also, who have heard the word of truth, the gospel of your salvation, and have believed in him, were sealed with the promised holy Spirit.

Ephesians 1:13

And do not grieve the holy Spirit of God, with which you were sealed for the day of redemption.

Ephesians 4:30

Jesus Is Your . . .
Abundance ✍

Moreover, God is able to make every grace abundant for you, so that in all things, always having all you need, you may have an abundance for every good work.

2 Corinthians 9:8

My God will fully supply whatever you need, in accord with his glorious riches in Christ Jesus.

Philippians 4:19

Therefore I tell you, all that you ask for in prayer, believe that you will receive it and it shall be yours.

Mark 11:24

Not that of ourselves we are qualified to take credit for anything as coming from us; rather, our qualification comes from God.

2 Corinthians 3:5

I have the strength for everything through him who empowers me.

Philippians 4:13

And what is the surpassing greatness of his power for us who believe, in accord with the exercise of his great might.

Ephesians 1:19

But he said to me, "My grace is sufficient for you, for power is made perfect in weakness." I will rather boast most gladly of my weaknesses, in order that the power of Christ may dwell with me.

2 Corinthians 12:9

No, in all these things we conquer overwhelmingly through him who loved us.

Romans 8:37

And whatever you ask in my name, I will do, so that the Father may be glorified in the Son.

John 14:13

On that day you will not question me about anything. Amen, amen, I say to you, whatever you ask the Father in my name he will give you. Until now you have not asked anything in my name; ask and you will receive, so that your joy may be complete.

John 16:23-24

Whatever you ask for in prayer with faith, you will receive.

Matthew 21:22

He who did not spare his own Son but handed him over for us all, how will he not also give us everything else along with him?

Romans 8:32

Bless the LORD, my soul;
　　do not forget all the gifts of God,
Who pardons all your sins,
　　heals all your ills,
Delivers your life from the pit,
　　surrounds you with love and compassion.

Psalm 103:2-4

Jesus Is Your . . .
Fulfillment

Blessed are they who hunger and thirst for
      righteousness,
   for they will be satisfied.

Matthew 5:6

   Find your delight in the LORD
who will give you your heart's desire.

Psalm 37:4

You shall eat and be filled,
     and shall praise the name of the LORD,
       your God,
Because he has dealt wondrously with you; my
    people shall nevermore be put to shame.

Joel 2:26

   Jesus said to them, "I am the bread of life;
whoever comes to me will never hunger, and
whoever believes in me will never thirst."

John 6:35

   Jesus answered and said to her, "Everyone who
drinks this water will be thirsty again; but whoever
drinks the water I shall give will never thirst; the

water I shall give will become in him a spring of water welling up to eternal life."

John 4:13-14

Why spend your money for what
        is not bread;
   your wages for what fails to satisfy?
Heed me, and you shall eat well,
   you shall delight in rich fare.

Isaiah 55:2

I will lavish choice portions upon the priests,
   and my people shall be filled with my blessings,
says the LORD.

Jeremiah 31:14

He who did not spare his own Son but handed him over for us all, how will he not also give us everything else along with him?

Romans 8:32

Jesus Is Your . . .
Everything ॐ

My God will fully supply whatever you need, in accord with his glorious riches in Christ Jesus.

Philippians 4:19

I have the strength for everything through him who empowers me.

Philippians 4:13

If you remain in me and my words remain in you, ask for whatever you want and it will be done for you.

John 15:7

On that day you will not question me about anything. Amen, amen, I say to you, whatever you ask the Father in my name he will give you. Until now you have not asked anything in my name; ask and you will receive, so that your joy may be complete.

John 16:23-24

Whatever you ask for in prayer with faith, you will receive.

Matthew 21:22

Therefore I tell you, all that you ask for in prayer, believe that you will receive it and it shall be yours.

Mark 11:24

Blessed be the God and Father of our Lord Jesus Christ, who has blessed us in Christ with every spiritual blessing in the heavens.

Ephesians 1:3

Beloved, if [our] hearts do not condemn us, we have confidence in God and receive from him whatever we ask, because we keep his commandments and do what pleases him.

1 John 3:21-22

For to me life is Christ, and death is gain.

Philippians 1:21

Moreover, God is able to make every grace abundant for you, so that in all things, always having all you need, you may have an abundance for every good work.

2 Corinthians 9:8

The Bible Is Your . . .
Law for Living ✍

All scripture is inspired by God and is useful for teaching, for refutation, for correction, and for training in righteousness.

2 Timothy 3:16

Know this first of all, that there is no prophecy of scripture that is a matter of personal interpretation, for no prophecy ever came through human will; but rather human beings moved by the holy Spirit spoke under the influence of God.

2 Peter 1:20-21

Indeed, the word of God is living and effective, sharper than any two-edged sword, penetrating even between soul and spirit, joints and marrow, and able to discern reflections and thoughts of the heart.

Hebrews 4:12

You search the scriptures, because you think you have eternal life through them; even they testify on my behalf.

John 5:39

You have been born anew, not from perishable but from imperishable seed, through the living and abiding word of God.

1 Peter 1:23

Your word, LORD, stands forever;
    it is firm as the heavens.

Psalm 119:89

Where is the wise one? Where is the scribe? Where is the debater of this age? Has not God made the wisdom of the world foolish?

1 Corinthians 1:20

Heaven and earth will pass away, but my words will not pass away.

Mark 13:31

The Bible Is Your . . .
Promise of Salvation ✍

The Spirit itself bears witness with our spirit that we are children of God, and if children, then heirs, heirs of God and joint heirs with Christ, if only we suffer with him so that we may also be glorified with him.

Romans 8:16-17

In my Father's house there are many dwelling places. If there were not, would I have told you that I am going to prepare a place for you? And if I go and prepare a place for you, I will come back again and take you to myself, so that where I am you also may be.

John 14:2-3

But now they desire a better homeland, a heavenly one. Therefore, God is not ashamed to be called their God, for he has prepared a city for them.

Hebrews 11:16

Then the king will say to those on his right, 'Come, you who are blessed by my Father. Inherit the kingdom prepared for you from the foundation of the world.'

Matthew 25:34

Blessed be the God and Father of our Lord Jesus Christ, who in his great mercy gave us a new birth to a living hope through the resurrection of Jesus Christ from the dead, to an inheritance that is imperishable, undefiled, and unfading, kept in heaven for you

1 Peter 1:3-4

But as it is written:
"What eye has not seen, and ear has not heard,
    and what has not entered the human heart,
    what God has prepared for those who
        love him."

1 Corinthians 2:9

Whatever you do, do from the heart, as for the Lord and not for others, knowing that you will receive from the Lord the due payment of the inheritance; be slaves of the Lord Christ.

Colossians 3:23-24

The Bible Is Your . . .
Guide for Life ✍

Your word is a lamp for my feet,
　　a light for my path.

Psalm 119:105

How can the young walk without fault?
　　Only by keeping your words.

Psalm 119:9

Jesus then said to those Jews who believed in him, "If you remain in my word, you will truly be my disciples, and you will know the truth, and the truth will set you free."

John 8:31-32

Through these, he has bestowed on us the precious and very great promises, so that through them you may come to share in the divine nature, after escaping from the corruption that is in the world because of evil desire.

2 Peter 1:4

I will instruct you and show you the way
　　you should walk,
　　give you counsel and watch over you.

Psalm 32:8

Even as he promised through the mouth
of his holy
prophets from of old:
to shine on those who sit in darkness and
death's shadow,
to guide our feet into the path of peace.

Luke 1:70, 79

Keep this book of the law on your lips. Recite it by day and by night, that you may observe carefully all that is written in it; then you will successfully attain your goal.

Joshua 1:8

All scripture is inspired by God and is useful for teaching, for refutation, for correction, and for training in righteousness, so that one who belongs to God may be competent, equipped for every good work.

2 Timothy 3:16-17

The Bible Is Your . . .
Stability ✍

Heaven and earth will pass away, but my words will not pass away.

Matthew 24:35

Your word, LORD, stands forever;
    it is firm as the heavens.

Psalm 119:89

Though the grass withers and the flower wilts,
    the word of our God stands forever.

Isaiah 40:8

My son, to my words be attentive,
to my sayings incline your ear;
Let them not slip out of your sight,
keep them within your heart;
For they are life to those who find them,
to man's whole being they are health.

Proverbs 4:20-22

What then shall we say to this? If God is for us, who can be against us?

Romans 8:31

God is our refuge and our strength,
an ever-present help in distress.

Psalm 46:1

The name of the LORD is a strong tower;
the just man runs to it and is safe.

Proverbs 18:10

But the Lord is faithful; he will strengthen you and guard you from the evil one.

2 Thessalonians 3:3

To the one who is able to keep you from stumbling and to present you unblemished and exultant, in the presence of his glory, to the only God, our savior, through Jesus Christ our Lord be glory, majesty, power, and authority from ages past, now, and for ages to come. Amen.

Jude 1:24-25

The Bible Is Your . . .
Strength ॐ

For thus said the Lord GOD,
    the Holy One of Israel:
By waiting and by calm you shall be saved,
    in quiet and in trust your strength lies.
    But this you did not wish.

Isaiah 30:15

They that hope in the LORD will renew
    their strength,
    they will soar as with eagles' wings;
They will run and not grow weary,
    walk and not grow faint.

Isaiah 40:31

I have the strength for everything through him
who empowers me.

Philippians 4:13

Fear not, I am with you;
    be not dismayed; I am your God.
I will strengthen you, and help you,
    and uphold you with my right hand
        of justice.

Isaiah 41:10

He gives strength to the fainting;
　　for the weak he makes vigor abound.

Isaiah 40:29

LORD, my rock, my fortress, my deliverer,
My God, my rock of refuge,
　　my shield, my saving
　　　horn, my stronghold!

Psalm 18:3

Therefore, put on the armor of God, that you may be able to resist on the evil day and, having done everything, to hold your ground.

Ephesians 6:13

The LORD is my light and my salvation;
　　whom do I fear?
The LORD is my life's refuge;
　　of whom am I afraid?

Psalm 27:1

Finally, draw your strength from the Lord and from his mighty power.

Ephesians 6:10

What to Do When You Feel . . .
Discouraged ✍

Have no anxiety at all, but in everything, by prayer and petition, with thanksgiving, make your requests known to God. Then the peace of God that surpasses all understanding will guard your hearts and minds in Christ Jesus.

Finally, brothers, whatever is true, whatever is honorable, whatever is just, whatever is pure, whatever is lovely, whatever is gracious, if there is any excellence and if there is anything worthy of praise, think about these things.

Philippians 4:6-8

Though I walk in the midst of dangers,
    you guard my life when my enemies rage.
You stretch out your hand;
    your right hand saves me.

Psalm 138:7

Do not let your hearts be troubled. You have faith in God; have faith also in me.

John 14:1

Peace I leave with you; my peace I give to you. Not as the world gives do I give it to you. Do not let your hearts be troubled or afraid.

John 14:27

We are afflicted in every way, but not constrained; perplexed, but not driven to despair; persecuted, but not abandoned; struck down, but not destroyed;

2 Corinthians 4:8-9

Therefore, do not throw away your confidence; it will have great recompense. You need endurance to do the will of God and receive what he has promised.

Hebrews 10:35-36

I am confident of this, that the one who began a good work in you will continue to complete it until the day of Christ Jesus.

Philippians 1:6

Let us not grow tired of doing good, for in due time we shall reap our harvest, if we do not give up.

Galatians 6:9

What to Do When You Feel . . .
Worried ✍

Cast all your worries upon him because he cares for you.

1 Peter 5:7

Do not let your hearts be troubled. You have faith in God; have faith also in me.

John 14:1

Have no anxiety at all, but in everything, by prayer and petition, with thanksgiving, make your requests known to God. Then the peace of God that surpasses all understanding will guard your hearts and minds in Christ Jesus.

Philippians 4:6-7

A nation of firm purpose you keep in peace;
in peace, for its trust in you.

Isaiah 26:3

My God will fully supply whatever you need, in accord with his glorious riches in Christ Jesus.

Philippians 4:19

When you lie down, you need not be afraid,
   when you rest, your sleep will be sweet.

Proverbs 3:24

Lovers of your teaching have much peace;
   for them there is no stumbling block.

Psalm 119:165

You who dwell in the shelter of the
      Most High,
   who abide in the shadow of the Almighty,
Say to the LORD, "My refuge and fortress,
   my God in whom I trust."

Psalm 91:1-2

Peace I leave with you; my peace I give to you.
Not as the world gives do I give it to you. Do not let
your hearts be troubled or afraid.

John 14:27

What to Do When You Feel . . .
Lonely ✍

Go, therefore, and make disciples of all nations, baptizing them in the name of the Father, and of the Son, and of the holy Spirit, teaching them to observe all that I have commanded you. And behold, I am with you always, until the end of the age.

Matthew 28:19-20

For the sake of his own great name the LORD will not abandon his people, since the LORD himself chose to make you his people.

1 Samuel 12:22

Fear not, I am with you;
    be not dismayed; I am your God.
I will strengthen you, and help you,
    and uphold you with my right
        hand of justice.

Isaiah 41:10

I will not leave you orphans; I will come to you.

John 14:18

Do not let your hearts be troubled. You have

faith in God; have faith also in me.

John 14:1

Since the LORD, your God, is a merciful God, he will not abandon and destroy you, nor forget the covenant which under oath he made with your fathers.

Deuteronomy 4:31

Even if my father and mother forsake me,
    the LORD will take me in.

Psalm 27:10

Though the mountains leave their place
    and the hills be shaken,
My love shall never leave you
    nor my covenant of peace be shaken,
    says the LORD, who has mercy on you.

Isaiah 54:10

Cast all your worries upon him because he cares for you.

1 Peter 5:7

God is our refuge and our strength,
an ever-present help in distress.

Psalm 46:2

What to Do When You Feel . . .
Depressed ✍

When you pass through the water, I will be
        with you;
    in the rivers you shall not drown.
When you walk through fire, you shall not be
        burned;
    the flames shall not consume you.

Isaiah 43:2

Beloved, do not be surprised that a trial by fire
is occurring among you, as if something strange
were happening to you. But rejoice to the extent
that you share in the sufferings of Christ, so that
when his glory is revealed you may also rejoice
exultantly.

1 Peter 4:12, 13

They that hope in the LORD will
    renew their strength,
  they will soar as with eagles' wings;
They will run and not grow weary,
  walk and not grow faint.

Isaiah 40:31

Blessed be the God and Father of our Lord

Jesus Christ, the Father of compassion and God of all encouragement, who encourages us in our every affliction, so that we may be able to encourage those who are in any affliction with the encouragement with which we ourselves are encouraged by God.

2 Corinthians 1:3-4

For I am convinced that neither death, nor life, nor angels, nor principalities, nor present things, nor future things, nor powers, nor height, nor depth, nor any other creature will be able to separate us from the love of God in Christ Jesus our Lord.

Romans 8:38-39

Finally, brothers, whatever is true, whatever is honorable, whatever is just, whatever is pure, whatever is lovely, whatever is gracious, if there is any excellence and if there is anything worthy of praise, think about these things.

Philippians 4:8

Fear not, I am with you;
    be not dismayed; I am your God.
I will strengthen you, and help you,
    and uphold you with my right
        hand of justice.

Isaiah 41:10

So humble yourselves under the mighty hand of God, that he may exalt you in due time. Cast all your worries upon him because he cares for you.

1 Peter 5:6-7

Those whom the LORD has ransomed will
    return
  and enter Zion singing,
  crowned with everlasting joy;
They will meet with joy and gladness, sorrow
  and mourning will flee.

Isaiah 51:11

What to Do When You Feel . . .
Dissatisfied ॐ

I will pour out water upon the thirsty ground,
  and streams upon the dry land;
I will pour out my spirit upon your offspring,
  and my blessing upon your descendants.

Isaiah 44:3

Trust in the LORD and do good
  that you may dwell in the land and
    live secure.

Psalm 37:3

I know indeed how to live in humble circumstances; I know also how to live with abundance. In every circumstance and in all things I have learned the secret of being well fed and of going hungry, of living in abundance and of being in need. I have the strength for everything through him who empowers me.

Philippians 4:12-13

From the fruit of his words a man
  has his fill of good things,
  and the work of his hands comes
    back to reward him.

Proverbs 12:14

And my people shall be filled with my
    blessings,
says the LORD.

Jeremiah 31:14b

You shall eat and be filled,
    and shall praise the name of the LORD,
        your God,
Because he has dealt wondrously with you;
    my people shall nevermore be put to
        shame.

Joel 2:26

For he satisfied the thirsty,
    filled the hungry with good things.

Psalm 107:9

Moreover, God is able to make every grace
abundant for you, so that in all things, always
having all you need, you may have an abundance
for every good work.

2 Corinthians 9:8

Blessed are they who hunger and thirst for
    righteousness,
    for they will be satisfied.

Matthew 5:6

What to Do When You Feel . . .
Condemned ✍

Hence, now there is no condemnation for those who are in Christ Jesus.

Romans 8:1

So whoever is in Christ is a new creation: the old things have passed away; behold, new things have come.

2 Corinthians 5:17

For God did not send his Son into the world to condemn the world, but that the world might be saved through him. Whoever believes in him will not be condemned, but whoever does not believe has already been condemned, because he has not believed in the name of the only Son of God.

John 3:17-18

Amen, amen, I say to you, whoever hears my word and believes in the one who sent me has eternal life and will not come to condemnation, but has passed from death to life.

John 5:24

For I will forgive their evildoing

and remember their sins no more.

Hebrews 8:12

It is I, I, who wipe out,
>   for my own sake, your offenses;
>   your sins I remember no more.

Isaiah 43:25

If we acknowledge our sins, he is faithful and just and will forgive our sins and cleanse us from every wrongdoing.

1 John 1:9

Happy the sinner whose fault is removed,
>   whose sin is forgiven.

Psalm 32:1

Then Jesus straightened up and said to her, "Woman, where are they? Has no one condemned you?" She replied, "No one, sir." Then Jesus said, "Neither do I condemn you. Go, [and] from now on do not sin any more."

John 8:10-11

Let us approach with a sincere heart and in absolute trust, with our hearts sprinkled clean from an evil conscience and our bodies washed in pure water.

Hebrews 10:22

What to Do When You Feel . . .
Confused ❧

For God did not give us a spirit of cowardice but rather of power and love and self-control.

2 Timothy 1:7

Beloved, do not be surprised that a trial by fire is occurring among you, as if something strange were happening to you. But rejoice to the extent that you share in the sufferings of Christ, so that when his glory is revealed you may also rejoice exultantly.

1 Peter 4:12-13

But if any of you lacks wisdom, he should ask God who gives to all generously and ungrudgingly, and he will be given it.

James 1:5

I will instruct you and show you the way you should walk,
give you counsel and watch over you.

Psalm 32:8

Lovers of your teaching have much peace;
for them there is no stumbling block.

Psalm 119:165

Cast your care upon the LORD,
    who will give you support.
God will never allow
    the righteous to stumble.

Psalm 55:23

He gives strength to the fainting;
    for the weak he makes vigor abound.

Isaiah 40:29

Have no anxiety at all, but in everything, by prayer and petition, with thanksgiving, make your requests known to God. Then the peace of God that surpasses all understanding will guard your hearts and minds in Christ Jesus.

Philippians 4:6-7

What to Do When You Feel . . .
Tempted ❦

Therefore, whoever thinks he is standing secure should take care not to fall. No trial has come to you but what is human. God is faithful and will not let you be tried beyond your strength; but with the trial he will also provide a way out, so that you may be able to bear it.

1 Corinthians 10:12-13

Because he himself was tested through what he suffered, he is able to help those who are being tested.

Hebrews 2:18

For sin is not to have any power over you, since you are not under the law but under grace.

Romans 6:14

In my heart I treasure your promise,
    that I may not sin against you.

Psalm 119:11

No one experiencing temptation should say, "I am being tempted by God"; for God is not subject to temptation to evil, and he himself tempts no one.

Rather, each person is tempted when he is lured and enticed by his own desire.

James 1:13-14

He who conceals his sins prospers not,
  but he who confesses and forsakes them
    obtains mercy.

Proverbs 28:13

If we acknowledge our sins, he is faithful and just and will forgive our sins and cleanse us from every wrongdoing.

1 John 1:9

Be sober and vigilant. Your opponent the devil is prowling around like a roaring lion looking for [someone] to devour. Resist him, steadfast in faith, knowing that your fellow believers throughout the world undergo the same sufferings.

1 Peter 5:8-9

Finally, draw your strength from the Lord and from his mighty power. Put on the armor of God so that you may be able to stand firm against the tactics of the devil. In all circumstances, hold faith as a shield, to quench all [the] flaming arrows of the evil one.

Ephesians 6:10-11, 16

Consider it all joy, my brothers, when you encounter various trials, for you know that the testing of your faith produces perseverance. Blessed is the man who perseveres in temptation, for when he has been proved he will receive the crown of life that he promised to those who love him.

James 1:2-3,12

What to Do When You Feel . . .
Angry ✒

Know this, my dear brothers: everyone should be quick to hear, slow to speak, slow to wrath, for the wrath of a man does not accomplish the righteousness of God.

James 1:19-20

Be angry but do not sin; do not let the sun set on your anger.

Ephesians 4:26

A mild answer calms wrath,
   but a harsh word stirs up anger.
Proverbs 15:1

If you forgive others their transgressions, your heavenly Father will forgive you.

Matthew 6:14

The patient man shows much good sense,
   but the quick-tempered man displays folly
      at its height.
Proverbs 14:29

Beloved, do not look for revenge but leave

room for the wrath; for it is written, "Vengeance is mine, I will repay, says the Lord."

Romans 12:19

If your enemy be hungry, give him food to eat,
    if he be thirsty, give him to drink;
For live coals you will heap on his head,
    and the LORD will vindicate you.

Proverbs 25:21-22

All bitterness, fury, anger, shouting, and reviling must be removed from you, along with all malice. [And] be kind to one another, compassionate, forgiving one another as God has forgiven you in Christ.

Ephesians 4:31-32

The wise man is cautious and shuns evil;
    the fool is reckless and sure of himself.
The quick-tempered man makes a fool of
        himself,
    but the prudent man is at peace.

Proverbs 14:16-17

Give up your anger, abandon your wrath;
    do not be provoked; it brings only harm.

Psalm 37:8

What to Do When You Feel . . .
Rebellious ✍

Obey your leaders and defer to them, for they keep watch over you and will have to give an account, that they may fulfill their task with joy and not with sorrow, for that would be of no advantage to you.

Hebrews 13:17

Therefore, gird up the loins of your mind, live soberly, and set your hopes completely on the grace to be brought to you at the revelation of Jesus Christ. Like obedient children, do not act in compliance with the desires of your former ignorance.

1 Peter 1:13-14

If you are willing, and obey,
  you shall eat the good things of the land;
But if you refuse and resist,
  the sword shall consume you:
  for the mouth of the LORD has spoken!

Isaiah 1:19-20

Be subject to every human institution for the Lord's sake, whether it be to the king as supreme or to governors as sent by him for the punishment of evildoers and the approval of those who do good. For it is the will of God that by doing good you may silence the ignorance of foolish people.

1 Peter 2:13-15

Son though he was, he learned obedience from what he suffered.

Hebrews 5:8

Be subordinate to one another out of reverence for Christ.

Ephesians 5:21

So I declare and testify in the Lord that you must no longer live as the Gentiles do, in the futility of their minds; darkened in understanding, alienated from the life of God because of their ignorance, because of their hardness of heart.

Ephesians 4:17-18

For you were once darkness, but now you are light in the Lord. Live as children of light,

Ephesians 5:8

So submit yourselves to God. Resist the devil, and he will flee from you.

James 4:7

What to Do When You Are . . .
Experiencing Fear ✍

For God did not give us a spirit of cowardice but rather of power and love and self-control.

2 Timothy 1:7

For you did not receive a spirit of slavery to fall back into fear, but you received a spirit of adoption, through which we cry, *Abba*, "Father!"

Romans 8:15

There is no fear in love, but perfect love drives out fear because fear has to do with punishment, and so one who fears is not yet perfect in love.

1 John 4:18

You who dwell in the shelter of the Most High,
    who abide in the shadow of the Almighty.

Psalm 91:1

In you I trust, I do not fear.
    What can mere mortals do to me?

Psalm 56:12

Even when I walk through a dark valley,
    I fear no harm for you are at my side;

your rod and staff give me courage.

You set a table before me
    as my enemies watch;
You anoint my head with oil;
    my cup overflows.

Psalm 23:4-5

Be strong and take heart,
    all you who hope in the LORD.

Psalm 31:25

Peace I leave with you; my peace I give to you.
Not as the world gives do I give it to you. Do not let
your hearts be troubled or afraid.

John 14:27

The LORD is my light and my salvation;
    whom do I fear?
The LORD is my life's refuge;
    of whom am I afraid?
Though an army encamp against me,
    my heart does not fear;
Though war be waged against me,
    even then do I trust.

Psalm 27:1, 3

What to Do When You Are . . .
Emotionally Distraught ❧

Fear not, I am with you;
    be not dismayed; I am your God.
I will strengthen you, and help you,
    and uphold you with my right hand
        of justice.

Isaiah 41:10

For where jealousy and selfish ambition exist, there is disorder and every foul practice. But the wisdom from above is first of all pure, then peaceable, gentle, compliant, full of mercy and good fruits, without inconstancy or insincerity. And the fruit of righteousness is sown in peace for those who cultivate peace.

James 3:16-18

The Lord GOD is my help,
  therefore I am not disgraced;
I have set my face like flint,
  knowing that I shall not be put to shame.

Isaiah 50:7

Cast your care upon the LORD,
  who will give you support.

God will never allow
the righteous to stumble.

Psalm 55:23

Have no anxiety at all, but in everything, by prayer and petition, with thanksgiving, make your requests known to God. Then the peace of God that surpasses all understanding will guard your hearts and minds in Christ Jesus.

Philippians 4:6-7

Lovers of your teaching have much peace;
for them there is no stumbling block.

Psalm 119:165

When you pass through the water, I will be
with you;
in the rivers you shall not drown.
When you walk through fire, you shall not be
burned;
the flames shall not consume you.

Isaiah 43:2

Finally, brothers, whatever is true, whatever is honorable, whatever is just, whatever is pure, whatever is lovely, whatever is gracious, if there is any excellence and if there is anything worthy of praise, think about these things.

Philippians 4:8

What to Do When You Are . . . in Need of Courage ✒

Wait for the LORD, take courage;
be stouthearted, wait for the LORD!

Psalm 27:14

Beloved, do not be surprised that a trial by fire is occurring among you, as if something strange were happening to you. But rejoice to the extent that you share in the sufferings of Christ, so that when his glory is revealed you may also rejoice exultantly.

1 Peter 4:12-13

For I am convinced that neither death, nor life, nor angels, nor principalities, nor present things, nor future things, nor powers, nor height, nor depth, nor any other creature will be able to separate us from the love of God in Christ Jesus our Lord.

Romans 8:38-39

Fear not, I am with you;
be not dismayed; I am your God.
I will strengthen you, and help you,
and uphold you with my right hand of justice.

Isaiah 41:10

I shall not die but live
and declare the deeds of the LORD.

Psalm 118:17

I have the strength for everything through him
who empowers me.

Philippians 4:13

Be strong and take heart,
all you who hope in the LORD.

Psalm 31:25

They that hope in the LORD will renew their
strength,
they will soar as with eagles' wings;
They will run and not grow weary,
walk and not grow faint.

Isaiah 40:31

What to Do When You Are . . .
in Need of Patience ⮥

In contrast, the fruit of the Spirit is love, joy, peace, patience, kindness, generosity, faithfulness, gentleness, self-control. Against such there is no law.

Galatians 5:22-23

Wait for the LORD, take courage;
  be stouthearted, wait for the LORD!

Psalm 27:14

It is good to hope in silence
  for the saving help of the LORD.

Lamentations 3:26

Be still before the LORD;
  wait for God.
Do not be provoked by the prosperous,
  nor by malicious schemers.

Psalm 37:7

Therefore, since we are surrounded by so great a cloud of witnesses, let us rid ourselves of every burden and sin that clings to us and persevere in running the race that lies before us.

Hebrews 12:1

For whatever was written previously was written for our instruction, that by endurance and by the encouragement of the scriptures we might have hope. May the God of endurance and encouragement grant you to think in harmony with one another, in keeping with Christ Jesus.

Romans 15:4-5

For you know that the testing of your faith produces perseverance. And let perseverance be perfect, so that you may be perfect and complete, lacking in nothing.

James 1:3-4

Be patient, therefore, brothers, until the coming of the Lord. See how the farmer waits for the precious fruit of the earth, being patient with it until it receives the early and the late rains. You too must be patient. Make your hearts firm, because the coming of the Lord is at hand.

James 5:7-8

What to Do When You Are . . .
in Need of Peace ❧

Peace I leave with you; my peace I give to you. Not as the world gives do I give it to you. Do not let your hearts be troubled or afraid.

John 14:27

Therefore, since we have been justified by faith, we have peace with God through our Lord Jesus Christ.

Romans 5:1

O LORD, you mete out peace to us,
 for it is you who have accomplished all we
  have done.

Isaiah 26:12

The concern of the flesh is death, but the concern of the spirit is life and peace.

Romans 8:6

Lovers of your teaching have much peace;
 for them there is no stumbling block.

Psalm 119:165

For the kingdom of God is not a matter of food

and drink, but of righteousness, peace, and joy in the holy Spirit; whoever serves Christ in this way is pleasing to God and approved by others. Let us then pursue what leads to peace and to building up one another.

Romans 14:17-19

Finally, brothers, rejoice. Mend your ways, encourage one another, agree with one another, live in peace, and the God of love and peace will be with you.

2 Corinthians 13:11

May the God of hope fill you with all joy and peace in believing, so that you may abound in hope by the power of the holy Spirit.

Romans 15:13

What to Do When You Are . . .
Lukewarm Spiritually ✍

Be watchful and strengthen what is left, which is going to die, for I have not found your works complete in the sight of my God. I know your works; I know that you are neither cold nor hot. I wish you were either cold or hot. So, because you are lukewarm, neither hot nor cold, I will spit you out of my mouth.

Revelation 3:2, 15-16

However, take care and be earnestly on your guard not to forget the things which your own eyes have seen, nor let them slip from your memory as long as you live, but teach them to your children and to your children's children.

Deuteronomy 4:9

Take care, brothers, that none of you may have an evil and unfaithful heart, so as to forsake the living God. Encourage yourselves daily while it is still "today," so that none of you may grow hardened by the deceit of sin.

Hebrews 3:12-13

About this we have much to say, and it is

difficult to explain, for you have become sluggish in hearing. Although you should be teachers by this time, you need to have someone teach you again the basic elements of the utterances of God. You need milk, [and] not solid food.

Hebrews 5:11-12

See to it that no one be deprived of the grace of God, that no bitter root spring up and cause trouble, through which many may become defiled,

Hebrews 12:15

Thus says the LORD:
Stand beside the earliest roads,
    ask the pathways of old
Which is the way to good, and walk it;
    thus you will find rest for your souls.
    But they said, "We will not walk it."

Jeremiah 6:16

Since the days of your fathers you have turned aside
    from my statutes, and have not kept them.
Return to me, and I will return to you,
    says the LORD of hosts.
Yet you say, "How must we return?"

Malachi 3:7

What to Do When You Are . . .
Grieving ✍

For the LORD comforts his people
    and shows mercy to his afflicted.

Isaiah 49:13b

When you pass through the water, I will be
        with you;
    in the rivers you shall not drown.
When you walk through fire, you shall not be
        burned;
    the flames shall not consume you.

Isaiah 43:2

Blessed are they who mourn,
    for they will be comforted.

Matthew 5:4

Blessed be the God and Father of our Lord
Jesus Christ, the Father of compassion and God of
all encouragement, who encourages us in our
every affliction, so that we may be able to
encourage those who are in any affliction with the
encouragement with which we ourselves are
encouraged by God.

2 Corinthians 1:3-4

Cast all your worries upon him because he cares for you.

1 Peter 5:7

Where, O death, is your victory?
Where, O death, is your sting?"
The sting of death is sin, and the power of sin is the law. But thanks be to God who gives us the victory through our Lord Jesus Christ.

1 Corinthians 15:55-57

Even when I walk through a dark valley,
I fear no harm for you are at my side;
your rod and staff give me courage.

Psalm 23:4

Fear not, I am with you;
be not dismayed; I am your God.
I will strengthen you, and help you,
and uphold you with my right hand
of justice.

Isaiah 41:10

He will wipe every tear from their eyes, and there shall be no more death or mourning, wailing or pain, [for] the old order has passed away.

Revelation 21:4

What to Do When You Are . . .
Doubting God ✍

Jesus said to them in reply, "Have faith in God. Amen, I say to you, whoever says to this mountain, 'Be lifted up and thrown into the sea,' and does not doubt in his heart but believes that what he says will happen, it shall be done for him. Therefore I tell you, all that you ask for in prayer, believe that you will receive it and it shall be yours."

Mark 11:22-24

As for you, do not seek what you are to eat and what you are to drink, and do not worry anymore. All the nations of the world seek for these things, and your Father knows that you need them. Instead, seek his kingdom, and these other things will be given you besides.

Luke 12:29-31

The one who calls you is faithful, and he will also accomplish it.

1 Thessalonians 5:24

The Lord does not delay his promise, as some regard "delay," but he is patient with you, not wishing that any should perish but that all should come to repentance.

2 Peter 3:9

God's way is unerring;
    the LORD's promise is tried and true;
    he is a shield for all who trust in him.

Psalm 18:31

Lo, the hand of the LORD is not too short to
    save,
nor his ear too dull to hear.

Isaiah 59:1

Beloved, do not be surprised that a trial by fire is occurring among you, as if something strange were happening to you. But rejoice to the extent that you share in the sufferings of Christ, so that when his glory is revealed you may also rejoice exultantly.

1 Peter 4:12-13

What to Do When . . .
You Need Confidence ☙

I have the strength for everything through him who empowers me.

Philippians 4:13

Thus we may say with confidence:
"The Lord is my helper,
[and] I will not be afraid.
What can anyone do to me?"

Hebrews 13:6

I am confident of this, that the one who began a good work in you will continue to complete it until the day of Christ Jesus.

Philippians 1:6

No, in all these things we conquer overwhelmingly through him who loved us.

Romans 8:37

And we have this confidence in him, that if we ask anything according to his will, he hears us. And if we know that he hears us in regard to whatever we ask, we know that what we have asked him for is ours.

1 John 5:14-15

When you pass through the water, I will be
    with you;
  in the rivers you shall not drown.
When you walk through fire, you shall not be
    burned;
  the flames shall not consume you.

Isaiah 43:2

For the LORD will be your confidence,
  and will keep your foot from the snare.

Proverbs 3:26

I rejoice, because I have confidence in you in
every respect.

2 Corinthians 7:16

Beloved, if [our] hearts do not condemn us, we
have confidence in God.

1 John 3:21

They that hope in the LORD will renew their
    strength,
  they will soar as with eagles' wings;
They will run and not grow weary,
  walk and not grow faint.

Isaiah 40:31

What to Do When . . .
You Have Troubles in Your Life ➤

The LORD is good,
> a refuge on the day of distress;
He takes care of those who have recourse to
> him.

Nahum 1:7

We are afflicted in every way, but not constrained; perplexed, but not driven to despair; persecuted, but not abandoned; struck down, but not destroyed.

2 Corinthians 4:8-9

Though I walk in the midst of dangers,
> you guard my life when my enemies rage.
You stretch out your hand;
> your right hand saves me.

Psalm 138:7

Do not let your hearts be troubled. You have faith in God; have faith also in me.

John 14:1

We know that all things work for good for those who love God, who are called according to his purpose.

Romans 8:28

I raise my eyes toward the mountains.
    From where will my help come?
My help comes from the LORD,
    the maker of heaven and earth.

Psalm 121:1-2

Cast all your worries upon him because he cares for you.

1 Peter 5:7

Do not worry about tomorrow; tomorrow will take care of itself. Sufficient for a day is its own evil.

Matthew 6:34

What to Do When . . .
You Have A
Physical Sickness ✍

Beloved, I hope you are prospering in every respect and are in good health, just as your soul is prospering.

3 John 2

Jesus went around to all the towns and villages, teaching in their synagogues, proclaiming the gospel of the kingdom, and curing every disease and illness.

Matthew 9:35

Everyone in the crowd sought to touch him because power came forth from him and healed them all.

Luke 6:19

He himself bore our sins in his body upon the cross, so that, free from sin, we might live for righteousness. By his wounds you have been healed.

1 Peter 2:24

But he was pierced for our offenses,

crushed for our sins,
Upon him was the chastisement that makes us
whole,
by his stripes we were healed.

Isaiah 53:5

Heal me, LORD, that I may be healed;
save me, that I may be saved,
for it is you whom I praise.

Jeremiah 17:14

"If you really listen to the voice of the LORD, your God," he told them, "and do what is right in his eyes: if you heed his commandments and keep all his precepts, I will not afflict you with any of the diseases with which I afflicted the Egyptians; for I, the LORD, am your healer."

Exodus 15:26

Is anyone among you sick? He should summon the presbyters of the church, and they should pray over him and anoint [him] with oil in the name of the Lord, and the prayer of faith will save the sick person, and the Lord will raise him up. If he has committed any sins, he will be forgiven.

James 5:14-15

What to Do When . . .
You Have
Financial Troubles ✍

Beloved, I hope you are prospering in every respect and are in good health, just as your soul is prospering.

3 John 2

Neither in my youth, nor now in old age
    have I ever seen the just abandoned
    or their children begging bread.

Psalm 37:25

Fear the LORD, you holy ones;
    nothing is lacking to those who fear him.

Psalm 34:10

The LORD is my shepherd;
    there is nothing I lack.

Psalm 23:1

Give and gifts will be given to you; a good measure, packed together, shaken down, and overflowing, will be poured into your lap. For the measure with which you measure will in return be measured out to you.

Luke 6:38

On the first day of the week each of you should set aside and save whatever one can afford, so that collections will not be going on when I come.

1 Corinthians 16:2

Cure the sick, raise the dead, cleanse lepers, drive out demons. Without cost you have received; without cost you are to give.

Matthew 10:8

Consider this: who ever sows sparingly will also reap sparingly, and whoever sows bountifully will also reap bountifully. Each must do as already determined, without sadness or compulsion, for God loves a cheerful giver. Moreover, God is able to make every grace abundant for you, so that in all things, always having all you need, you may have an abundance for every good work.

2 Corinthians 9:6-8

Keep this book of the law on your lips. Recite it by day and by night, that you may observe carefully all that is written in it; then you will successfully attain your goal.

Joshua 1:8

So do not worry and say, 'What are we to eat?' or 'What are we to drink?' or 'What are we to wear?' All these things the pagans seek. Your heavenly Father knows that you need them all. But seek first the kingdom [of God] and his righteousness, and all these things will be given you besides.

Matthew 6:31-33

My God will fully supply whatever you need, in accord with his glorious riches in Christ Jesus.

Philippians 4:19

What to Do When . . .
You Have
Marital Problems ࣔ

The LORD God said: "It is not good for the man to be alone. I will make a suitable partner for him."

Genesis 2:18

That is why a man leaves his father and mother and clings to his wife, and the two of them become one body.

Genesis 2:24

So [also] husbands should love their wives as their own bodies. He who loves his wife loves himself. For no one hates his own flesh but rather nourishes and cherishes it, even as Christ does the church, because we are members of his body.

"For this reason a man shall leave [his] father
and [his] mother
and be joined to his wife,
and the two shall become one flesh."

This is a great mystery, but I speak in reference to Christ and the church. In any case, each one of you should love his wife as himself, and the wife should respect her husband.

Ephesians 5:28-33

Every man should have his own wife, and every woman her own husband. The husband should fulfill his duty toward his wife, and likewise the wife toward her husband. A wife does not have authority over her own body, but rather her husband, and similarly a husband does not have authority over his own body, but rather his wife. Do not deprive each other, except perhaps by mutual consent for a time, to be free for prayer, but then return to one another, so that Satan may not tempt you through your lack of self-control.

1 Corinthians 7:2-5

Love does no evil to the neighbor; hence, love is the fulfillment of the law.

Romans 13:10

Finally, all of you, be of one mind, sympathetic, loving toward one another, compassionate, humble. Do not return evil for evil, or insult for insult; but, on the contrary, a blessing, because to this you were called, that you might inherit a blessing. For:
   "Whoever would love life
      and see good days

must keep the tongue from evil
    and the lips from speaking deceit,
must turn from evil and do good,
    seek peace and follow after it."

1 Peter 3:8-11

Trust in the LORD with all your heart,
    on your own intelligence rely not;
In all your ways be mindful of him,
    and he will make straight your paths.

Proverbs 3:5-6

Hatred stirs up disputes,
    but love covers all offenses.

Proverbs 10:12

Since you have purified yourselves by obedience to the truth for sincere mutual love, love one another intensely from a [pure] heart.

1 Peter 1:22

What to Do When . . .
You Are Deserted
by Loved Ones ✍

The LORD is a stronghold for the oppressed,
   a stronghold in times of trouble.

Psalm 9:10

You, LORD, will not forsake your people,
   nor abandon your very own.

Psalm 94:14

Even if my father and mother forsake me,
   the LORD will take me in.

Psalm 27:10

Cast all your worries upon him because he
cares for you.

1 Peter 5:7

Neither in my youth, nor now in old age
   have I ever seen the just abandoned
   or their children begging bread.

Psalm 37:25

Since the LORD, your God, is a merciful God,
he will not abandon and destroy you, nor forget the

covenant which under oath he made with your fathers.

Deuteronomy 4:31

Can a mother forget her infant,
> be without tenderness for the child of her
> > womb?

Even should she forget,
> I will never forget you.

See, upon the palms of my hands I have written
> your name;
> your walls are ever before me.

Isaiah 49:15-16

For the sake of his own great name the LORD will not abandon his people, since the LORD himself chose to make you his people.

1 Samuel 12:22

What to Do When . . .
You Don't Understand God's Ways ✒

For my thoughts are not your thoughts,
nor are your ways my ways, says the
LORD.
As high as the heavens are above the earth,
so high are my ways above your ways
and my thoughts above your thoughts.
Isaiah 55:8-9

What then shall we say to this? If God is for us, who can be against us?

Romans 8:31

What will separate us from the love of Christ? Will anguish, or distress, or persecution, or famine, or nakedness, or peril, or the sword? As it is written:
"For your sake we are being slain all the day;
we are looked upon as sheep to be
slaughtered."
No, in all these things we conquer overwhelmingly through him who loved us.

Romans 8:35-37

Fear not, I am with you;
be not dismayed; I am your God.
I will strengthen you, and help you,
and uphold you with my right hand of justice.

Isaiah 41:10

We know that all things work for good for those who love God, who are called according to his purpose.

Romans 8:28

God's way is unerring;
the LORD'S promise is tried and true;
he is a shield for all who trust in him.

Psalm 18:31

What to Do When . . .
You Are Waiting on God ✒

Wait for the LORD, take courage;
>> be stouthearted, wait for the LORD!

Psalm 27:14

My soul, be at rest in God alone,
>> from whom comes my hope.

Psalm 62:6

Our soul waits for the LORD,
>> who is our help and shield.

Psalm 33:20

They that hope in the LORD will renew their
>> strength,
>> they will soar as with eagles' wings;
They will run and not grow weary,
>> walk and not grow faint.

Isaiah 40:31

Let us hold unwaveringly to our confession that gives us hope, for he who made the promise is trustworthy.

Hebrews 10:23

I wait with longing for the LORD,
my soul waits for his word.

Psalm 130:5

On that day it will be said:
"Behold our God, to whom we looked to save us!
This is the LORD for whom we looked;
let us rejoice and be glad that he has saved us!"

Isaiah 25:9

What the Bible Has to Say About . . .
Faith ✍

Faith is the realization of what is hoped for and evidence of things not seen.

Hebrews 11:1

Thus faith comes from what is heard, and what is heard comes through the word of Christ.

Romans 10:17

For by the grace given to me I tell everyone among you not to think of himself more highly than one ought to think, but to think soberly, each according to the measure of faith that God has apportioned.

Romans 12:3

Therefore, since we are surrounded by so great a cloud of witnesses, let us rid ourselves of every burden and sin that clings to us and perservere in running the race that lies before us while keeping our eyes fixed on Jesus, the leader and perfecter of faith. For the sake of the joy that lay before him he endured the cross, despising its shame, and has taken his seat at the right of the throne of God.

Hebrews 12:1-2

He said to them, "Because of your little faith.

Amen, I say to you, if you have faith the size of a mustard seed, you will say to this mountain, 'Move from here to there,' and it will move. Nothing will be impossible for you."

Matthew 17:20

But without faith it is impossible to please him, for anyone who approaches God must believe that he exists and that he rewards those who seek him.

Hebrews 11:6

For whoever is begotten by God conquers the world. And the victory that conquers the world is our faith.

1 John 5:4

When he entered the house, the blind men approached him and Jesus said to them, "Do you believe that I can do this?" "Yes, Lord," they said to him. Then he touched their eyes and said, "Let it be done for you according to your faith."

Matthew 9:28-29

Jesus said to him, "'If you can!' Everything is possible to one who has faith."

Mark 9:23

What the Bible Has to Say About . . .
Love ✍

Beloved, let us love one another, because love is of God; everyone who loves is begotten by God and knows God. Whoever is without love does not know God, for God is love.

1 John 4:7-8

In this is love: not that we have loved God, but that he loved us and sent his Son as expiation for our sins. Beloved, if God so loved us, we also must love one another. No one has ever seen God. Yet, if we love one another, God remains in us, and his love is brought to perfection in us.

1 John 4:10-12

As the Father loves me, so I also love you. Remain in my love. If you keep my commandments, you will remain in my love, just as I have kept my Father's commandments and remain in his love.

John 15:9-10

Whoever has my commandments and observes them is the one who loves me. And whoever loves me will be loved by my Father, and I will love him and reveal myself to him.

John 14:21

This is my commandment: love one another as I love you. No one has greater love than this, to lay down one's life for one's friends. You are my friends if you do what I command you. This I command you: love one another.

John 15:12-14, 17

The LORD appears to him from afar:
With age-old love I have loved you;
   so I have kept my mercy toward you.

Jeremiah 31:3

For the Father himself loves you, because you have loved me and have come to believe that I came from God.

John 16:27

For God so loved the world that he gave his only Son, so that everyone who believes in him might not perish but might have eternal life.

John 3:16

For I am convinced that neither death, nor life, nor angels, nor principalities, nor present things, nor future things, nor powers, nor height, nor depth, nor any other creature will be able to separate us from the love of God in Christ Jesus our Lord.

Romans 8:38-39

I give you a new commandment: love one another. As I have loved you, so you also should love one another. This is how all will know that you are my disciples, if you have love for one another.

John 13:34-35

What the Bible Has to Say About . . .
Eternity ☙

And this is the testimony: God gave us eternal life, and this life is in his Son.

1 John 5:11

Amen, amen, I say to you, whoever hears my word and believes in the one who sent me has eternal life and will not come to condemnation, but has passed from death to life.

John 5:24

For God so loved the world that he gave his only Son, so that everyone who believes in him might not perish but might have eternal life.

John 3:16

Amen, amen, I say to you, whoever believes has eternal life.

John 6:47

For the Father loves his Son and shows him everything that he himself does, and he will show him greater works than these, so that you may be amazed.

John 5:20

Only goodness and love will pursue me]
    all the days of my life;
I will dwell in the house of the LORD
    for years to come.

Psalm 23:6

Jesus told her, "I am the resurrection and the life; whoever believes in me, even if he dies, will live, and everyone who lives and believes in me will never die. Do you believe this?"

John 11:25-26

My sheep hear my voice; I know them, and they follow me. I give them eternal life, and they shall never perish. No one can take them out of my hand.

John 10:27-28

But whoever drinks the water I shall give will never thirst; the water I shall give will become in him a spring of water welling up to eternal life.

John 4:14

What the Bible Has to Say About ...
Praise ✍

Through him [then] let us continually offer God a sacrifice of praise, that is, the fruit of lips that confess his name.

Hebrews 13:15

Hallelujah!

How good to celebrate our God in song;
    how sweet to give fitting praise.

Psalm 147:1

'Praised be the LORD,' I exclaim,
    and I am safe from my enemies.

2 Samuel 22:4

I will bless the LORD at all times;
praise shall be always in my mouth.

Psalm 34:2

God mounts the throne amid shouts of joy;
    the LORD, amid trumpet blasts.
Sing praise to God, sing praise;
    sing praise to our king, sing praise.

Psalm 47:6-7

Great is the LORD and highly praised
    in the city of our God:
The holy mountain.

Psalm 48:2

Those who offer praise as a sacrifice honor me; to
    the obedient I will show the salvation of God.
Psalm 50:23

It is good to give thanks to the LORD,
    to sing praise to your name, Most High.
Psalm 92:1

What the Bible Has to Say About . . .
Serving God ✍

No one can serve two masters. He will either hate one and love the other, or be devoted to one and despise the other. You cannot serve God and mammon.

Matthew 6:24

The LORD, your God, you shall worship; then I will bless your food and drink, and I will remove all sickness from your midst; no woman in your land will be barren or miscarry; and I will give you a full span of life.

Exodus 23:25-26

And now, Israel, what does the LORD, your God, ask of you but to fear the LORD, your God, and follow his ways exactly, to love and serve the LORD, your God, with all your heart and all your soul.

Deuteronomy 10:12

If it does not please you to serve the LORD, decide today whom you will serve, the gods your fathers served beyond the River or the gods of the Amorites in whose country you are dwelling. As for me and my household, we will serve the LORD.

Joshua 24:15

But now we are released from the law, dead to what held us captive, so that we may serve in the newness of the spirit and not under the obsolete letter.

Romans 7:6

Shout joyfully to the LORD, all you lands;
 worship the LORD with cries of gladness;
 come before him with joyful song.
Enter the temple gates with praise,
 its courts with thanksgiving.
Give thanks to God, bless his name;

Psalm 100:1-2,4

What the Bible Has to Say About . . .
Obedience ❧

This rather is what I commanded them: Listen to my voice; then I will be your God and you shall be my people. Walk in all the ways that I command you, so that you may prosper.

Jeremiah 7:23

If you love me, you will keep my commandments. Whoever has my commandments and observes them is the one who loves me. And whoever loves me will be loved by my Father, and I will love him and reveal myself to him.

John 14:15, 21

But Peter and the apostles said in reply, "We must obey God rather than men."

Acts 5:29

And if you follow me by keeping my statutes and commandments, as your father David did, I will give you a long life.

1 Kings 3:14

Teach me to do your will,
  for you are my God.
May your kind spirit guide me
  on ground that is level.

Psalm 143:10

Children, obey your parents [in the Lord], for this is right.

Ephesians 6:1

Children, obey your parents in everything, for this is pleasing to the Lord. Fathers, do not provoke your children, so they may not become discouraged. Slaves, obey your human masters in everything, not only when being watched, as currying favor, but in simplicity of heart, fearing the Lord. Whatever you do, do from the heart, as for the Lord and not for others, knowing that you will receive from the Lord the due payment of the inheritance; be slaves of the Lord Christ.

Colossians 3:20-24

What the Bible Has to Say About . . .
Bodily Lust ✒

The concern of the flesh is death, but the concern of the spirit is life and peace. For the concern of the flesh is hostility toward God; it does not submit to the law of God, nor can it; and those who are in the flesh cannot please God.

Romans 8:6-8

Because the one who sows for his flesh will reap corruption from the flesh, but the one who sows for the spirit will reap eternal life from the spirit.

Galatians 6:8

Adulterers! Do you not know that to be a lover of the world means enmity with God? Therefore, whoever wants to be a lover of the world makes himself an enemy of God.

James 4:4

To satisfy the one who recruited him, a soldier does not become entangled in the business affairs of life. So turn from youthful desires and pursue righteousness, faith, love, and peace, along with those who call on the Lord with purity of heart.

2 Timothy 2:4, 22

Beloved, I urge you as aliens and sojourners to keep away from worldly desires that wage war against the soul.

1 Peter 2:11

I urge you therefore, brothers, by the mercies of God, to offer your bodies as a living sacrifice, holy and pleasing to God, your spiritual worship. Do not conform yourselves to this age but be transformed by the renewal of your mind, that you may discern what is the will of God, what is good and pleasing and perfect.

Romans 12:1-2

Finally, brothers, whatever is true, whatever is honorable, whatever is just, whatever is pure, whatever is lovely, whatever is gracious, if there is any excellence and if there is anything worthy of praise, think about these things.

Philippians 4:8

Think of what is above, not of what is on earth.

Colossians 3:2

What the Bible Has to Say About . . .
the Grace of God ✍

Grace and favor you granted me,
   and your providence has preserved my spirit.

Job 10:12

Then all who take refuge in you will be glad and
      forever shout for joy.
Protect them that you may be the joy
   of those who love your name.

Psalm 5:12

The LORD remembers us and will bless us,
      will bless the house of Israel,
      will bless the house of Aaron,
Will bless those who fear the LORD,
      small and great alike.

Psalm 115:12-13

Everything indeed is for you, so that the grace
bestowed in abundance on more and more people
may cause the thanksgiving to overflow for the
glory of God.

2 Corinthians 4:15

So let us confidently approach the throne of grace to receive mercy and to find grace for timely help.

Hebrews 4:16

What the Bible Has to Say About . . . the Holy Spirit ✍

Do you not know that your body is a temple of the holy Spirit within you, whom you have from God, and that you are not your own?

1 Corinthians 6:19

And I will ask the Father, and he will give you another Advocate to be with you always, the Spirit of truth, which the world cannot accept, because it neither sees nor knows it. But you know it, because it remains with you, and will be in you.

John 14:16-17

But I tell you the truth, it is better for you that I go. For if I do not go, the Advocate will not come to you. But if I go, I will send him to you. But when he comes, the Spirit of truth, he will guide you to all truth. He will not speak on his own, but he will speak what he hears, and will declare to you the things that are coming.

John 16:7, 13

I am baptizing you with water, for repentance, but the one who is coming after me is mightier than I. I am not worthy to carry his sandals. He will baptize you with the holy Spirit and fire.

Matthew 3:11

"Whoever believes in me, as scripture says:
'Rivers of living water will flow from within
              him.'"
He said this in reference to the Spirit that those
who came to believe in him were to receive. There
was, of course, no Spirit yet, because Jesus had not
yet been glorified.

John 7:38-39

And they were all filled with the holy Spirit and
began to speak in different tongues, as the Spirit
enabled them to proclaim.

Acts 2:4

Peter [said] to them, "Repent and be baptized,
every one of you, in the name of Jesus Christ for the
forgiveness of your sins; and you will receive the
gift of the holy Spirit."

Acts 2:38

As they prayed, the place where they were
gathered shook, and they were all filled with the
holy Spirit and continued to speak the word of God
with boldness.

Acts 4:31

What the Bible Has to Say About . . . God's Faithfulness ✍

As the bow appears in the clouds, I will see it and recall the everlasting covenant that I have established between God and all living beings — all mortal creatures that are on earth.

Genesis 9:16

Know that I am with you; I will protect you wherever you go, and bring you back to this land. I will never leave you until I have done what I promised you.

Genesis 28:15

"Blessed be the LORD who has given rest to his people Israel, just as he promised. Not a single word has gone unfulfilled of the entire generous promise he made through his servant Moses."

1 Kings 8:56

LORD, your love reaches to heaven;
   your fidelity, to the clouds.

Psalm 36:6

God is faithful, and by him you were called to fellowship with his Son, Jesus Christ our Lord.

1 Corinthians 1:9

No trial has come to you but what is human. God is faithful and will not let you be tried beyond your strength; but with the trial he will also provide a way out, so that you may be able to bear it.

1 Corinthians 10:13

The Lord does not delay his promise, as some regard "delay," but he is patient with you, not wishing that any should perish but that all should come to repentance.

2 Peter 3:9

What the Bible Has to Say About . . .
The Church ✍

He delivered us from the power of darkness and transferred us to the kingdom of his beloved Son.

He is the head of the body, the church.

He is the beginning, the firstborn from the dead,

that in all things he himself might be preeminent.

Colossians 1:13, 18

He said to them, "But who do you say that I am?" Simon Peter said in reply, "You are the Messiah, the Son of the living God." Jesus said to him in reply, "Blessed are you, Simon son of Jonah. For flesh and blood has not revealed this to you, but my heavenly Father. And so I say to you, you are Peter, and upon this rock I will build my church, and the gates of the netherworld shall not prevail against it."

Matthew 16:15-18

For this reason I kneel before the Father, from whom every family in heaven and on earth is named, to him be glory in the church and in Christ

Jesus to all generations, forever and ever. Amen.

Ephesians 3:14-15, 21

For as in one body we have many parts, and all the parts do not have the same function, so we, though many, are one body in Christ and individually parts of one another.

Romans 12:4-5

We ask you, brothers, to respect those who are laboring among you and who are over you in the Lord and who admonish you, and to show esteem for them with special love on account of their work. Be at peace among yourselves.

1 Thessalonians 5:12-13

Remember your leaders who spoke the word of God to you. Consider the outcome of their way of life and imitate their faith. Obey your leaders and defer to them, for they keep watch over you and will have to give an account, that they may fulfill their task with joy and not with sorrow, for that would be of no advantage to you.

Hebrews 13:7,17

What the Bible Has to Say About ...
Stewardship ᪥

Now in regard to the collection for the holy ones, you also should do as I ordered the churches of Galatia. On the first day of the week each of you should set aside and save whatever one can afford, so that collections will not be going on when I come.

1 Corinthians 16:1-2

Consider this: whoever sows sparingly will also reap sparingly, and whoever sows bountifully will also reap bountifully. Each must do as already determined, without sadness or compulsion, for God loves a cheerful giver. Moreover, God is able to make every grace abundant for you, so that in all things, always having all you need, you may have an abundance for every good work.

2 Corinthians 9:6-8

Whatever you do, do from the heart, as for the Lord and not for others, knowing that you will receive from the Lord the due payment of the inheritance; be slaves of the Lord Christ.

Colossians 3:23-24

But store up treasures in heaven, where neither moth nor decay destroys, nor thieves break in and steal. For where your treasure is, there also will your heart be.

Matthew 6:20-21

Give and gifts will be given to you; a good measure, packed together, shaken down, and overflowing, will be poured into your lap. For the measure with which you measure will in return be measured out to you.

Luke 6:38

But seek first the kingdom [of God] and his righteousness, and all these things will be given you besides.

Matthew 6:33

And everyone who has given up houses or brothers or sisters or father or mother or children or lands for the sake of my name will receive a hundred times more, and will inherit eternal life.

Matthew 19:29

Cure the sick, raise the dead, cleanse lepers, drive out demons. Without cost you have received; without cost you are to give.

Matthew 10:8

What the Bible Has to Say About . . .
Satan ♊

Be sober and vigilant. Your opponent the devil is prowling around like a roaring lion looking for [someone] to devour. Resist him, steadfast in faith.

1 Peter 5:8-9a

So submit yourselves to God. Resist the devil, and he will flee from you.

James 4:7

He delivered us from the power of darkness and transferred us to the kingdom of his beloved Son.

Colossians 1:13

They conquered him by the blood of the Lamb
and by the word of their testimony;
love for life did not deter them from death.
Revelation 12:11

Beloved, do not trust every spirit but test the spirits to see whether they belong to God, because many false prophets have gone out into the world. This is how you can know the Spirit of God: every spirit that acknowledges Jesus Christ come in the flesh be longs to God, and every spirit that does not acknowledge Jesus does not belong to God. This is the spirit of the antichrist that, as you heard, is to come, but in fact is already in the world. You belong to God, children, and you have conquered them, for the one who is in you is greater than the one who is in the world.

1 John 4:1-4

These signs will accompany those who believe: in my name they will drive out demons, they will speak new languages. They will pick up serpents [with their hands], and if they drink any deadly thing, it will not harm them. They will lay hands on the sick, and they will recover.

Mark 16:17-18

But if it is by the Spirit of God that I drive out demons, then the kingdom of God has come upon you. How can anyone enter a strong man's house and steal his property, unless he first ties up the strong man? Then he can plunder his house.

Matthew 12:28-29

Whoever sins belongs to the devil, because the devil has sinned from the beginning. Indeed, the Son of God was revealed to destroy the works of the devil.

1 John 3:8

Then the God of peace will quickly crush Satan under your feet. The grace of our Lord Jesus be with you.

Romans 16:20

I am writing to you, fathers, because you know him who is from the beginning.

I am writing to you, young men, because you have conquered the evil one.

I write to you, children, because you know the Father.

I write to you, fathers, because you know him who is from the beginning.

I write to you, young men, because you are strong and the word of God remains in you, and you have conquered the evil one.

1 John 2:13-14

What the Bible Has to Say About . . . the Return of Christ ❧

Behold, I tell you a mystery. We shall not all fall asleep, but we will all be changed, in an instant, in the blink of an eye, at the last trumpet. For the trumpet will sound, the dead will be raised incorruptible, and we shall be changed. For that which is corruptible must clothe itself with incorruptibility, and that which is mortal must clothe itself with immortality. And when this which is corruptible clothes itself with incorruptibility and this which is mortal clothes itself with immortality, then the word that is written shall come about:

"Death is swallowed up in victory.

Where, O death, is your victory?

Where, O death, is your sting?"

The sting of death is sin, and the power of sin is the law. But thanks be to God who gives us the victory through our Lord Jesus Christ.

1 Corinthians 15:51-57

They said, "Men of Galilee, why are you standing there looking at the sky? This Jesus who has been taken up from you into heaven will return in the same way as you have seen him going into heaven."

Acts 1:11

Beloved, we are God's children now; what we shall be has not yet been revealed. We do know that when it is revealed we shall be like him, for we shall see him as he is. Everyone who has this hope based on him makes himself pure, as he is pure.

1 John 3:2-3

"There will be signs in the sun, the moon, and the stars, and on earth nations will be in dismay, perplexed by the roaring of the sea and the waves. People will die of fright in anticipation of what is coming upon the world, for the powers of the heavens will be shaken. And then they will see the Son of Man coming in a cloud with power and great glory. But when these signs begin to happen, stand erect and raise your heads because your redemption is at hand."

Luke 21:25-28

"For just as lightning comes from the east and is seen as far as the west, so will the coming of the Son of Man be.

"Immediately after the tribulation of those days,

the sun will be darkened,
and the moon will not give its light,
and the stars will fall from the sky,
and the powers of the heavens will be
shaken.

And then the sign of the Son of Man will appear in heaven, and all the tribes of the earth will mourn, and they will see the Son of Man coming upon the clouds of heaven with power and great glory. And he will send out his angels with a trumpet blast, and they will gather his elect from the four winds, from one end of the heavens to the other."

Matthew 24:27, 29-31

"But of that day and hour no one knows, neither the angels of heaven, nor the Son, but the Father alone. For as it was in the days of Noah, so it will be at the coming of the Son of Man. In [those] days before the flood, they were eating and drinking, marrying and giving in marriage, up to the day that Noah entered the ark. They did not know until the flood came and carried them all away. So will it be [also] at the coming of the Son of Man. Two men will be out in the field; one will be taken, and one will be left. Two women will be grinding at the mill; one will be taken, and one will be left. Therefore, stay awake! For you do not know on which day your Lord will come. Be sure of this: if the master of the house had known the hour of night when the thief was coming, he would have stayed awake and not let his house be broken into. So too, you also must be prepared, for at an hour you do not expect, the Son of Man will come."

Matthew 24:36-44

But understand this: there will be terrifying times in the last days. People will be self-centered and lovers of money, proud, haughty, abusive, disobedient to their parents, ungrateful, irreligious, callous, implacable, slanderous, licentious, brutal, hating what is good, traitors, reckless, conceited, lovers of pleasure rather than lovers of God, as they make a pretense of religion but deny its power. Reject them.

2 Timothy 3:1-5

In the same way, when you see all these things, know that he is near, at the gates.

Matthew 24:33

"Do not let your hearts be troubled. You have faith in God; have faith also in me. In my Father's house there are many dwelling places. If there were not, would I have told you that I am going to prepare a place for you? And if I go and prepare a place for you, I will come back again and take you to myself, so that where I am you also may be. Where [I] am going you know the way."

John 14:1-4

What the Bible Has to Say About . . .
Sinners ﾑ

All have sinned and are deprived of the glory of God.

Romans 3:23

Therefore, just as through one person sin entered the world, and through sin, death, and thus death came to all, inasmuch as all sinned.

Romans 5:12

But God proves his love for us in that while we were still sinners Christ died for us.

Romans 5:8

For God did not send his Son into the world to condemn the world, but that the world might be saved through him.

John 3:17

I have not come to call the righteous to repentance but sinners.

Luke 5:32

For the Son of Man has come to seek and to save what was lost.

Luke 19:10

Jesus answered and said to him, "Amen, amen, I say to you, no one can see the kingdom of God without being born from above."

John 3:3

For God so loved the world that he gave his only Son, so that everyone who believes in him might not perish but might have eternal life.

John 3:16

And they said, "Believe in the Lord Jesus and you and your household will be saved."

Acts 16:31

He said to them, "Go into the whole world and proclaim the gospel to every creature. Whoever believes and is baptized will be saved; whoever does not believe will be condemned."

Mark 16:15-16

"The Spirit of the Lord is upon me,
   because he has anointed me
      to bring glad tidings to the poor.
He has sent me to proclaim liberty to captives
   and recovery of sight to the blind,
      to let the oppressed go free,
and to proclaim a year acceptable to the Lord."

Luke 4:18-19

Truth from the Bible About . . .
Forgiving Others ✍

If you forgive others their transgressions, your heavenly Father will forgive you. But if you do not forgive others, neither will your Father forgive your transgressions.

Matthew 6:14-15

Then Peter approaching asked him, "Lord, if my brother sins against me, how often must I forgive him? As many as seven times?" Jesus answered, "I say to you, not seven times but seventy-seven times."

Matthew 18:21-22

Be on your guard! If your brother sins, rebuke him; and if he repents, forgive him.

Luke 17:3

When you stand to pray, forgive anyone against whom you have a grievance, so that your heavenly Father may in turn forgive you your transgressions.

Mark 11:25

Blessed are they who are persecuted for the

sake of righteousness,
for theirs is the kingdom of heaven.

Blessed are you when they insult you and persecute you and utter every kind of evil against you [falsely] because of me. Rejoice and be glad, for your reward will be great in heaven. Thus they persecuted the prophets who were before you.

Matthew 5:10-12

But I say to you, love your enemies, and pray for those who persecute you.

Matthew 5:44

Do not return evil for evil, or insult for insult; but, on the contrary, a blessing, because to this you were called, that you might inherit a blessing. For:
"Whoever would love life
    and see good days
must keep the tongue from evil
    and the lips from speaking deceit..."

1 Peter 3:9-10

All bitterness, fury, anger, shouting, and reviling must be removed from you, along with all malice. [And] be kind to one another, compassionate, forgiving one another as God has forgiven you in Christ.

Ephesians 4:31-32

Truth from the Bible About . . .
Community ✍

What we have seen and heard
>we proclaim now to you,
>so that you too may have fellowship with us;
>for our fellowship is with the Father
>and with his Son, Jesus Christ.

But if we walk in the light as he is in the light, then we have fellowship with one another, and the blood of his Son Jesus cleanses us from all sin.

1 John 1:3, 7

And live in love, as Christ loved us and handed himself over for us as a sacrificial offering to God for a fragrant aroma . . . addressing one another [in] psalms and hymns and spiritual songs, singing and playing to the Lord in your hearts...because we are members of his body.

Ephesians 5:2, 19, 30

Let the word of Christ dwell in you richly, as in all wisdom you teach and admonish one another, singing psalms, hymns, and spiritual songs with gratitude in your hearts to God.

Colossians 3:16

That their hearts may be encouraged as they are brought together in love, to have all the richness of fully assured understanding, for the knowledge of the mystery of God, Christ.

Colossians 2:2

Now that very day two of them were going to a village seven miles from Jerusalem called Emmaus, and they were conversing about all the things that had occurred. And it happened that while they were conversing and debating, Jesus himself drew near and walked with them.

Luke 24:13-15

You, whose company I enjoyed,
　　at whose side I walked
　　in procession in the house of God.

Psalm 55:15

I urge you, brothers, in the name of our Lord Jesus Christ, that all of you agree in what you say, and that there be no divisions among you, but that you be united in the same mind and in the same purpose.

1 Corinthians 1:10

Bear one another's burdens, and so you will fulfill the law of Christ. So then, while we have the opportunity, let us do good to all, but especially to those who belong to the family of the faith.

Galatians 6:2, 10

So then you are no longer strangers and sojourners, but you are fellow citizens with the holy ones and members of the household of God, built upon the foundation of the apostles and prophets, with Christ Jesus himself as the capstone. Through him the whole structure is held together and grows into a temple sacred in the Lord; in him you also are being built together into a dwelling place of God in the Spirit.

Ephesians 2:19-22

If there is any encouragement in Christ, any solace in love, any participation in the Spirit, any compassion and mercy, complete my joy by being of the same mind, with the same love, united in heart, thinking one thing.

Philippians 2: 1-2

We must consider how to rouse one another to love and good works. We should not stay away from our assembly, as is the custom of some, but encourage one another, and this all the more as you see the day drawing near.

Hebrews 10:24-25

Truth from the Bible About ...
Your Responsibility ✍

He said to them, "Go into the whole world and proclaim the gospel to every creature."

Mark 16:15

But you will receive power when the holy Spirit comes upon you, and you will be my witnesses in Jerusalem, throughout Judea and Samaria, and to the ends of the earth.

Acts 1:8

You are the salt of the earth. But if salt loses its taste, with what can it be seasoned? It is no longer good for anything but to be thrown out and trampled underfoot. You are the light of the world. A city set on a mountain cannot be hidden. Nor do they light a lamp and then put it under a bushel basket; it is set on a lampstand, where it gives light to all in the house. Just so, your light must shine before others, that they may see your good deeds and glorify your heavenly Father.

Matthew 5:13-16

And whoever gives only a cup of cold water to one of these little ones to drink because he is a disciple — amen, I say to you, he will surely not lose his reward.

Matthew 10:42

For God is not unjust so as to overlook your work and the love you have demonstrated for his name by having served and continuing to serve the holy ones.

Hebrews 6:10

Religion that is pure and undefiled before God and the Father is this: to care for orphans and widows in their affliction and to keep oneself unstained by the world.

James 1:27

If a brother or sister has nothing to wear and has no food for the day, and one of you says to them, "Go in peace, keep warm, and eat well," but you do not give them the necessities of the body, what good is it? So also faith of itself, if it does not have works, is dead.

James 2:15-17

And the crowds asked him, "What then should we do?" He said to them in reply, "Whoever has two cloaks should share with the person who has

none. And whoever has food should do likewise."
Luke 3:10-11

Take to heart these words which I enjoin on you today. Drill them into your children. Speak of them at home and abroad, whether you are busy or at rest. Bind them at your wrist as a sign and let them be as a pendant on your forehead. Write them on the doorposts of your houses and on your gates.
Deuteronomy 6:6-9

And whoever does not provide for relatives and especially family members has denied the faith and is worse than an unbeliever.
1 Timothy 5:8

"Therefore, take these words of mine into your heart and soul. Bind them at your wrist as a sign, and let them be a pendant on your forehead. Teach them to your children, speaking of them at home and abroad, whether you are busy or at rest."
Deuteronomy 11:18-19

Truth from the Bible About . . .
Speaking God's Word ॐ

Amen, I say to you, whoever says to this mountain, 'Be lifted up and thrown into the sea,' and does not doubt in his heart but believes that what he says will happen, it shall be done for him.

Mark 11:23

The Lord replied, "If you have faith the size of a mustard seed, you would say to [this] mulberry tree, 'Be uprooted and planted in the sea,' and it would obey you."

Luke 17:6

He woke up, rebuked the wind, and said to the sea, "Quiet! Be still!" The wind ceased and there was great calm.

Mark 4:39

By faith we understand that the universe was ordered by the word of God, so that what is visible came into being through the invisible.

Hebrews 11:3

Because I did not speak on my own, but the Father who sent me commanded me what to say and speak.

And I know that his commandment is eternal life. So what I say, I say as the Father told me.

John 12:49-50

If anyone thinks he is religious and does not bridle his tongue but deceives his heart, his religion is vain.

James 1:26

"The word is near you,
     in your mouth and in your heart"
(that is, the word of faith that we preach), for, if you confess with your mouth that Jesus is Lord and believe in your heart that God raised him from the dead, you will be saved. For one believes with the heart and so is justified, and one confesses with the mouth and so is saved.

Romans 10:8-10

Let us hold unwaveringly to our confession that gives us hope, for he who made the promise is trustworthy.

Hebrews 10:23

Since, then, we have the same spirit of faith, according to what is written, "I believed, therefore I spoke," we too believe and therefore speak.

2 Corinthians 4:13

Truth from the Bible About . . .
Finding the Will of God ☙

But if any of you lacks wisdom, he should ask God who gives to all generously and ungrudgingly, and he will be given it.

James 1:5

Your word is a lamp for my feet,
a light for my path.

Psalm 119:105

Keep this book of the law on your lips. Recite it by day and by night, that you may observe carefully all that is written in it; then you will successfully attain your goal.

Joshua 1:8

You are my rock and my fortress;
for your name's sake lead and guide me.

Psalm 31:4

Trust in the LORD with all your heart,
on your own intelligence rely not;
In all your ways be mindful of him,
and he will make straight your paths.

Proverbs 3:5-6

But when he comes, the Spirit of truth, he will guide you to all truth. He will not speak on his own, but he will speak what he hears, and will declare to you the things that are coming.

John 16:13

Truth from the Bible About . . .
Answered Prayer ೮೨

Before they call, I will answer;
> while they are yet speaking, I will hearken
> > to them.

Isaiah 65:24

Ask and it will be given to you; seek and you will find; knock and the door will be opened to you. For everyone who asks, receives; and the one who seeks, finds; and to the one who knocks, the door will be opened.

Matthew 7:7-8

Whatever you ask for in prayer with faith, you will receive.

Matthew 21:22

Again, [amen,] I say to you, if two of you agree on earth about anything for which they are to pray, it shall be granted to them by my heavenly Father. For where two or three are gathered together in my name, there am I in the midst of them.

Matthew 18:19-20

Therefore I tell you, all that you ask for in prayer, believe that you will receive it and it shall be yours.

Mark 11:24

And whatever you ask in my name, I will do, so that the Father may be glorified in the Son.

John 14:13

If you remain in me and my words remain in you, ask for whatever you want and it will be done for you.

John 15:7

On that day you will not question me about anything. Amen, amen, I say to you, whatever you ask the Father in my name he will give you.

John 16:23

All who call upon me I will answer;
   I will be with them in distress;
   I will deliver them and give them honor.

Psalm 91:15

But when you pray, go to your inner room, close the door, and pray to your Father in secret. And your Father who sees in secret will repay you.

Matthew 6:6

Truth from the Bible About . . .
Giving Good Example ✍

And they said, "Believe in the Lord Jesus and you and your household will be saved."

Acts 16:31

In just the same way, it is not the will of your heavenly Father that one of these little ones be lost.

Matthew 18:14

The Lord does not delay his promise, as some regard "delay," but he is patient with you, not wishing that any should perish but that all should come to repentance.

2 Peter 3:9

"Whoever causes one of these little ones who believe in me to sin, it would be better for him to have a great millstone hung around his neck and to be drowned in the depths of the sea. Woe to the world because of things that cause sin! Such things must come, but woe to the one through whom they come!"

Matthew 18:6-7

Test everything; retain what is good.

Refrain from every kind of evil.

1 Thessalonians 5:21-22

Cast your care upon the LORD,
    who will give you support.
God will never allow
    the righteous to stumble.

Psalm 55:23

But I tell you the truth, it is better for you that I go. For if I do not go, the Advocate will not come to you. But if I go, I will send him to you. And when he comes he will convict the world in regard to sin and righteousness and condemnation.

John 16:7-8

Truth from the Bible About . . .
Marriage ❧

The LORD God said: "It is not good for the man to be alone. I will make a suitable partner for him." That is why a man leaves his father and mother and clings to his wife, and the two of them become one body.

Genesis 2:18, 24

He who finds a wife finds happiness;
    it is a favor he receives from the LORD.

Proverbs 18:22

Take wives and beget sons and daughters; find wives for your sons and give your daughters husbands, so that they may bear sons and daughters. There you must increase in number, not decrease.

Jeremiah 29:6

But because of cases of immorality every man should have his own wife, and every woman her own husband. The husband should fulfill his duty toward his wife, and likewise the wife toward her husband. A wife does not have authority over her own body, but rather her husband, and similarly a husband does not have authority over his own body, but rather his wife.

1 Corinthians 7:2-4

So I would like younger widows to marry, have children, and manage a home, so as to give the adversary no pretext for maligning us.

1 Timothy 5:14

Let marriage be honored among all and the marriage bed be kept undefiled, for God will judge the immoral and adulterers.

Hebrews 13:4

So [also] husbands should love their wives as their own bodies. He who loves his wife loves himself. For no one hates his own flesh but rather nourishes and cherishes it, even as Christ does the church, because we are members of his body.
"For this reason a man shall leave [his] father
and [his] mother
and be joined to his wife,
and the two shall become one flesh."
This is a great mystery, but I speak in reference to Christ and the church. In any case, each one of you should love his wife as himself, and the wife should respect her husband.

Ephesians 5:28-33

Truth from the Bible About ...
Divorce ✎

"It was also said, 'Whoever divorces his wife must give her a bill of divorce.' But I say to you, whoever divorces his wife (unless the marriage is unlawful) causes her to commit adultery, and whoever marries a divorced woman commits adultery."

Matthew 5:31-32

The Pharisees approached and asked, "Is it lawful for a husband to divorce his wife?" They were testing him. He said to them in reply, "What did Moses command you?" They replied, "Moses permitted him to write a bill of divorce and dismiss her." But Jesus told them, "Because of the hardness of your hearts he wrote you this commandment. But from the beginning of creation, 'God made them male and female. For this reason a man shall leave his father and mother [and be joined to his wife], and the two shall become one flesh.' So they are no longer two but one flesh. Therefore what God has joined together, no human being must separate." In the house the disciples again questioned him about this. He said to them, "Whoever divorces his wife and marries another commits adultery against her; and if she divorces her husband and marries another, she commits adultery."

Mark 10:2-12

Everyone who divorces his wife and marries another commits adultery, and the one who marries a woman divorced from her husband commits adultery.

Luke 16:18

To the married, however, I give this instruction (not I, but the Lord): a wife should not separate from her husband — and if she does separate she must either remain single or become reconciled to her husband — and a husband should not divorce his wife.

To the rest I say (not the Lord): if any brother has a wife who is an unbeliever, and she is willing to go on living with him, he should not divorce her; and if any woman has a husband who is an unbeliever, and he is willing to go on living with her, she should not divorce her husband. For the unbelieving husband is made holy through his wife, and the unbelieving wife is made holy through the brother. Otherwise your children would be unclean, whereas in fact they are holy.

If the unbeliever separates, however, let him

separate. The brother or sister is not bound in such cases; God has called you to peace. For how do you know, wife, whether you will save your husband; or how do you know, husband, whether you will save your wife?

Only, everyone should live as the Lord has assigned, just as God called each one. I give this order in all the churches.

1 Corinthians 7:10-17

Truth from the Bible About . . .
Your Family 🕮

And they said, "Believe in the Lord Jesus and you and your household will be saved."

Acts 16:31

All bitterness, fury, anger, shouting, and reviling must be removed from you, along with all malice. [And] be kind to one another, compassionate, forgiving one another as God has forgiven you in Christ.

Ephesians 4:31-32

Train a boy in the way he should go;
>even when he is old, he will not swerve
>>from it.

Proverbs 22:6

"Honor your father and your mother, that you may have a long life in the land which the LORD, your God, is giving you."

Exodus 20:12

Children, pay heed to a father's right;
>do so that you may live.
For the LORD sets a father in honor

over his children;
a mother's authority he confirms
over her sons.
He who honors his father atones for sins;
he stores up riches who reveres
his mother.
He who honors his father is gladdened
by children,
and when he prays he is heard.
He who reveres his father will live a long life;
he obeys the LORD who brings comfort
to his mother.
He who fears the LORD honors his father,
and serves his parents as rulers.
In word and deed honor your father
that his blessing may come upon you;
For a father's blessing gives a
family firm roots,
but a mother's curse uproots the
growing plant.

Sirach 3:1-9

He must manage his own household well, keeping his children under control with perfect dignity; for if a man does not know how to manage his own household, how can he take care of the church of God?

1 Timothy 3:4-5

Grandchildren are the crown of old men,
and the glory of children is their parentage.

Proverbs 17:6

Correct your son, and he will bring you
comfort,
and give delight to your soul.

Proverbs 29:17

Fathers, do not provoke your children to anger,
but bring them up with the training and instruction
of the Lord.

Ephesians 6:4

The good man leaves an inheritance to his
children's children,
but the wealth of the sinner is stored up for the
just.

Proverbs 13:22

The father of a just man will exult with glee;
he who begets a wise son will have joy in
him.

Proverbs 23:24

All your sons shall be taught by the LORD,
and great shall be the peace of your children.

Isaiah 54:13

Truth from the Bible About . . .
Wives ๑

He who finds a wife finds happiness;
　　it is a favor he receives from the LORD.

Proverbs 18:22

Be not jealous of the wife of your bosom,
　　lest you teach her to do evil against you.

Sirach 9:1

Enjoy life with the wife whom you love, all the
days of the fleeting life that is granted you under
the sun. This is your lot in life, for the toil of your
labors under the sun.

Ecclesiastes 9:9

The husband should fulfill his duty toward his
wife, and likewise the wife toward her husband.

1 Corinthians 7:3

A worthy wife is the crown of her husband,
　　but a disgraceful one is like rot in his bones.

Proverbs 12:4

So [also] husbands should love their wives as

their own bodies. He who loves his wife loves himself. For no one hates his own flesh but rather nourishes and cherishes it, even as Christ does the church, because we are members of his body.

"For this reason a man shall leave [his] father
and [his] mother
and be joined to his wife,
and the two shall become one flesh."

This is a great mystery, but I speak in reference to Christ and the church. In any case, each one of you should love his wife as himself, and the wife should respect her husband.

Ephesians 5:28-33

When one finds a worthy wife,
her value is far beyond pearls.
Her husband, entrusting his heart to her,
has an unfailing prize.
She brings him good, and not evil,
all the days of her life.
She obtains wool and flax
and makes cloth with skillful hands.
Like merchant ships,
she secures her provisions from afar.
She rises while it is still night,
and distributes food to her household.
She picks out a field to purchase;
out of her earnings she plants a vineyard.

She is girt about with strength,
  and sturdy are her arms.
She enjoys the success of her dealings;
  at night her lamp is undimmed.
She puts her hands to the distaff,
  and her fingers ply the spindle.
She reaches out her hands to the poor,
  and extends her arms to the needy.
She fears not the snow for her household;
  all her charges are doubly clothed.
She makes her own coverlets;
  fine linen and purple are her clothing.
Her husband is prominent at the city gates
  as he sits with the elders of the land.
She makes garments and sells them,
  and stocks the merchants with belts.
She is clothed with strength and dignity,
  and she laughs at the days to come.
She opens her mouth in wisdom,
  and on her tongue is kindly counsel.
She watches the conduct of her household,
  and eats not her food in idleness.
Her children rise up and praise her;
  her husband, too, extols her:
"Many are the women of proven worth,
  but you have excelled them all."
Charm is deceptive and beauty fleeting;
  the woman who fears the LORD

is to be praised.
Give her a reward of her labors,
   and let her works praise her at the city gates.
Proverbs 31:10-31

Home and possessions are an inheritance from
                  parents,
but a prudent wife is from the LORD.
Proverbs 19:14

Truth from the Bible About . . .
Widows ✍

Religion that is pure and undefiled before God and the Father is this: to care for orphans and widows in their affliction and to keep oneself unstained by the world.

James 1:27

The blessing of those in extremity came
        upon me,
    and the heart of the widow I made joyful.

Job 29:13

The LORD protects the stranger,
    sustains the orphan and the widow,
    but thwarts the way of the wicked.

Psalm 146:9

Leave your orphans behind, I will keep
        them alive;
    your widows, let them trust in me.

Jeremiah 49:11

A wife is bound to her husband as long as he lives. But if her husband dies, she is free to be married to whomever she wishes, provided that it be in the Lord. She is more blessed, though, in my opinion, if she remains as she is, and I think that I too have the Spirit of God.

1 Corinthians 7:39-40

The LORD rebuilds Jerusalem,
  gathers the dispersed of Israel,
Heals the brokenhearted,
  binds up their wounds,

Psalm 147:2-3

So you also are now in anguish. But I will see you again, and your hearts will rejoice, and no one will take your joy away from you.

John 16:22

Truth from the Bible About . . .
Singles ✍

I will espouse you to me forever:
I will espouse you in right and in justice,
in love and in mercy.

Hosea 2:21

Now to the unmarried and to widows, I say: it
is a good thing for them to remain as they are, as I
do.

1 Corinthians 7:8

Only, everyone should live as the Lord has
assigned, just as God called each one. I give this
order in all the churches. Are you bound to a wife?
Do not seek a separation. Are you free of a wife?
Then do not look for a wife. If you marry, however,
you do not sin, nor does an unmarried woman sin
if she marries; but such people will experience
affliction in their earthly life, and I would like to
spare you that.

1 Corinthians 7:17, 27-28

I should like you to be free of anxieties. An
unmarried man is anxious about the things of the
Lord, how he may please the Lord. But a married

man is anxious about the things of the world, how he may please his wife . . . I am telling you this for your own benefit, not to impose a restraint upon you, but for the sake of propriety and adherence to the Lord without distraction.

1 Corinthians 7:32-33, 35

The one who stands firm in his resolve, however, who is not under compulsion but has power over his own will, and has made up his mind to keep his virgin, will be doing well.

1 Corinthians 7:37

Let marriage be honored among all and the marriage bed be kept undefiled, for God will judge the immoral and adulterers.

Hebrews 13:4

Find your delight in the LORD
who will give you your heart's desire.

Psalm 37:4

In the same way, my brothers, you also were put to death to the law through the body of Christ, so that you might belong to another, to the one who was raised from the dead in order that we might bear fruit for God.

Romans 7:4

Each one must examine his own work, and then he will have reason to boast with regard to himself alone, and not with regard to someone else.

Galatians 6:4

Truth from the Bible About . . .
The Elderly ॐ

Even to your old age I am the same,
   even when your hair is gray I will bear you;
It is I who have done this, I who will continue,
   and I who will carry you to safety.

Isaiah 46:4

God, you have taught me from my youth;
   to this day I proclaim your wondrous deeds.
Now that I am old and gray,
   do not forsake me, God,
That I may proclaim your might
   to all generations yet to come,
Your power.

Psalm 71:17-18

The glory of young men is their strength,
   and the dignity of old men is gray hair.

Proverbs 20:29

Gray hair is a crown of glory;
   it is gained by virtuous living.

Proverbs 16:31

For many days, and years of life,

and peace, will they bring you.

Proverbs 3:2

With length of days I will satisfy them
and show them my saving power.

Psalm 91:16

Neither in my youth, nor now in old age
have I ever seen the just abandoned
or their children begging bread.

Psalm 37:25

Let your life be free from love of money but be
content with what you have, for he has said, "I will
never forsake you or abandon you."

Hebrews 13:5

For what is our hope or joy or crown to boast of
in the presence of our Lord Jesus at his coming if
not you yourselves?

1 Thessalonians 2:19

Even when I walk through a dark valley,
I fear no harm for you are at my side;
your rod and staff give me courage.

Psalm 23:4

The afflicted and the needy seek water in vain,

their tongues are parched with thirst.
I, the LORD, will answer them;
I, the God of Israel, will not forsake them.

Isaiah 41:17

For I am convinced that neither death, nor life, nor angels, nor principalities, nor present things, nor future things, nor powers, nor height, nor depth, nor any other creature will be able to separate us from the love of God in Christ Jesus our Lord.

Romans 8:38-39

What You Can Do to . . .
Grow Spiritually 🙠

But grow in grace and in the knowledge of our Lord and savior Jesus Christ. To him be glory now and to the day of eternity. [Amen.]

2 Peter 3:18

Like newborn infants, long for pure spiritual milk so that through it you may grow into salvation, for you have tasted that the Lord is good.

1 Peter 2:2-3

Be diligent in these matters, be absorbed in them, so that your progress may be evident to everyone.

1 Timothy 4:15

Therefore, let us leave behind the basic teaching about Christ and advance to maturity, without laying the foundation all over again: repentance from dead works and faith in God.

Hebrews 6:1

For this reason I kneel before the Father, from whom every family in heaven and on earth is named, that he may grant you in accord with the riches of his glory to be strengthened with power through his Spirit in the inner self, and that Christ may dwell in your hearts through faith; that you, rooted and grounded in love, may have strength to comprehend with all the holy ones what is the breadth and length and height and depth, and to know the love of Christ that surpasses knowledge, so that you may be filled with all the fullness of God.

Ephesians 3:14-19

Let the word of Christ dwell in you richly, as in all wisdom you teach and admonish one another, singing psalms, hymns, and spiritual songs with gratitude in your hearts to God.

Colossians 3:16

All of us, gazing with unveiled face on the glory of the Lord, are being transformed into the same image from glory to glory, as from the Lord who is the Spirit.

2 Corinthians 3:18

I am confident of this, that the one who began a good work in you will continue to complete it until the day of Christ Jesus. And this is my prayer: that your love may increase ever more and more in knowledge and every kind of perception, to

discern what is of value, so that you may be pure
and blameless for the day of Christ.

Philippians 1:6, 9-10

So that we may no longer be infants, tossed by
waves and swept along by every wind of teaching
arising from human trickery, from their cunning in
the interests of deceitful scheming. Rather, living
the truth in love, we should grow in every way into
him who is the head, Christ.

Ephesians 4:14-15

What You Can Do to . . .
Change the World ✍

You are the light of the world. A city set on a mountain cannot be hidden. Nor do they light a lamp and then put it under a bushel basket; it is set on a lampstand, where it gives light to all in the house. Just so, your light must shine before others, that they may see your good deeds and glorify your heavenly Father.

Matthew 5:14-16

The Spirit of the Lord is upon me,
      because he has anointed me
            to bring glad tidings to the poor.
He has sent me to proclaim liberty to captives
      and recovery of sight to the blind,
            to let the oppressed go free.

Luke 4:18

Amen, amen, I say to you, whoever believes in me will do the works that I do, and will do greater ones than these, because I am going to the Father.

John 14:12

"And so I say to you, you are Peter, and upon this rock I will build my church, and the gates of the netherworld shall not prevail against it. I will give you the keys to the kingdom of heaven. Whatever you bind on earth shall be bound in heaven; and whatever you loose on earth shall be loosed in heaven."

Matthew 16:18-19

I give you a new commandment: love one another. As I have loved you, so you also should love one another. This is how all will know that you are my disciples, if you have love for one another.

John 13:34, 35

For whoever is begotten by God conquers the world. And the victory that conquers the world is our faith. Who [indeed] is the victor over the world but the one who believes that Jesus is the Son of God?

1 John 5:4-5

Faith is the realization of what is hoped for and evidence of things not seen. Because of it the ancients were well attested. By faith we understand that the universe was ordered by the word of God, so that what is visible came into being through the invisible.

Hebrews 11;1-3

You are the salt of the earth.

Matthew 5:13a

For God so loved the world that he gave his only Son, so that everyone who believes in him might not perish but might have eternal life.

John 3:16

"Go, therefore, and make disciples of all nations, baptizing them in the name of the Father, and of the Son, and of the holy Spirit, teaching them to observe all that I have commanded you. And behold, I am with you always, until the end of the age."

Matthew 28:19-20

What You Can Do to ...
Help Your Business 🔊

Beloved, I hope you are prospering in every respect and are in good health, just as your soul is prospering.

3 John 2

Remember then, it is the LORD, your God, who gives you the power to acquire wealth, by fulfilling, as he has now done, the covenant which he swore to your fathers.

Deuteronomy 8:18

Trust in the LORD with all your heart,
    on your own intelligence rely not;
In all your ways be mindful of him,
    and he will make straight your paths.
Be not wise in your own eyes,
    fear the LORD and turn away from evil;
This will mean health for your flesh
    and vigor for your bones.

Honor the LORD with your wealth,
    with first fruits of all your produce;
Then will your barns be filled with grain,

with new wine your vats will overflow.

Proverbs 3:5-10

But seek first the kingdom [of God] and his righteousness, and all these things will be given you besides.

Matthew 6:33

Entrust your works to the LORD,
   and your plans will succeed.

Proverbs 16:3

If they obey and serve him,
   they spend their days in prosperity,
   their years in happiness.

Job 36:11

Do not grow slack in zeal, be fervent in spirit, serve the Lord.

Romans 12:11

Nevertheless we urge you, brothers, to progress even more, and to aspire to live a tranquil life, to mind your own affairs, and to work with your [own] hands, as we instructed you, that you may conduct yourselves properly toward outsiders and not depend on anyone.

1 Thessalonians 4: 10b-12

What You Can Do to . . .
Please God ✍

When the trumpeters and singers were heard
as a single voice praising and giving thanks to the
LORD, and when they raised the sound of the
trumpets, cymbals and other musical instruments
to "give thanks to the LORD, for he is good, for his
mercy endures forever," the building of the LORD's
temple was filled with a cloud. The priests could
not continue to minister because of the cloud, since
the LORD's glory filled the house of God.

2 Chronicles 5:13-14

And, like living stones, let yourselves be built
into a spiritual house to be a holy priesthood to
offer spiritual sacrifices acceptable to God through
Jesus Christ. But you are "a chosen race, a royal
priesthood, a holy nation, a people of his own, so
that you may announce the praises" of him who
called you out of darkness into his wonderful light.

1 Peter 2:5, 9

Through him [then] let us continually offer God
a sacrifice of praise, that is, the fruit of lips that
confess his name. Do not neglect to do good and to

share what you have; God is pleased by sacrifices
of that kind.

Hebrews 13:15-16

"Worthy are you, Lord our God,
    to receive glory and honor and power,
for you created all things;
        because of your will they came to be and
            were created."

Revelation 4:11

But without faith it is impossible to please him,
for anyone who approaches God must believe that
he exists and that he rewards those who seek him.

Hebrews 11:6

My mouth will speak your praises, LORD;
    all flesh will bless your holy name forever.

Psalm 145:21

I will give fervent thanks to the LORD;
    before all I will praise my God.

Psalm 109:30

All you peoples, clap your hands;
    shout to God with joyful cries.

Psalm 47:2

God's Plan of . . .
Salvation ✍

Therefore, just as through one person sin entered the world, and through sin, death, and thus death came to all, inasmuch as all sinned.

Romans 5:12

For the wages of sin is death, but the gift of God is eternal life in Christ Jesus our Lord.

Romans 6:23

But God proves his love for us in that while we were still sinners Christ died for us.

Romans 5:8

For God did not send his Son into the world to condemn the world, but that the world might be saved through him.

John 3:17

Whoever believes in the Son has eternal life, but whoever disobeys the Son will not see life, but the wrath of God remains upon him.

John 3:36

For God so loved the world that he gave his

only Son, so that everyone who believes in him might not perish but might have eternal life.

John 3:16

But to those who did accept him he gave power to become children of God, to those who believe in his name.

John 1:12

For by grace you have been saved through faith, and this is not from you; it is the gift of God; it is not from works, so no one may boast.

Ephesians 2:8-9

Behold, I stand at the door and knock. If anyone hears my voice and opens the door, [then] I will enter his house and dine with him, and he with me.

Revelation 3:20

And this is the testimony: God gave us eternal life, and this life is in his Son. Whoever possesses the Son has life; whoever does not possess the Son of God does not have life.

I write these things to you so that you may know that you have eternal life, you who believe in the name of the Son of God.

1 John 5:11-13

Verses that Are Special to Me...

_____

_____

_____

_____

_____

_____

_____

_____

_____

_____

_____

_____

_____

_____

_____

_____

_____

_____

_____

_____

Verses that Are Special to Me...

_____
_____
_____
_____
_____
_____
_____
_____
_____
_____
_____
_____
_____
_____
_____
_____
_____
_____
_____
_____
_____